D1016090

"Mountaineers Books has a deserved reputation for solid, information-rich guidebooks, and *Snowshoe Routes: Oregon* is no exception ... Andersen also supplies an insightful touch and color that make it obvious from the details that he's flop-footed each of the routes."
—*Salem Statesman-Journal*

"If you want to snowshoe in Oregon, this is your book."
—*The Cascadian*

"*Snowshoe Routes: Oregon* is a clearly organized, concisely written, and informative guide to snowshoe routes covering the entirety of Oregon... [It] is a useful source for experienced snowshoers, yet is spun entertainingly for individuals interested in all types cof winter recreation."
—*Northwest Travel*

SNOWSHOE ROUTES

Oregon

SHEA ANDERSEN

THE
MOUNTAINEERS
BOOKS

 Published by
The Mountaineers Books
1001 SW Klickitat Way, Suite 201
Seattle, WA 98134

© 2001 by Shea Andersen

First printing 2001, second printing 2003, third printing 2005

Published simultaneously in Great Britain by Cordee, 3a DeMontfort Street, Leicester, England, LE1 7HD

Manufactured in the United States of America

Acquisitions Editor: Margaret Sullivan
Project Editor: Christine Ummel Hosler
Copy Editor: Karen Parkin
Series Cover and Book Design: The Mountaineers Books
Book Layout Artist: Dottie Martin
Cartographer: Jerry Painter
Photographer: Shea Andersen

Cover photograph: *Broken Top in the Three Sisters Wilderness, as seen from Tumalo Mountain*
Frontispiece: *Mount Bachelor from Vista Butte*

Library of Congress Cataloging-in-Publication Data
Andersen, Shea, 1972-
  Snowshoe routes, Oregon / Shea Andersen.— 1st ed.
    p. cm.
Includes index.
  ISBN 0-89886-833-5 (pbk.)
  1. Snowshoes and snowshoeing—Oregon—Guidebooks. 2.
Trails—Oregon—Guidebooks. 3. Oregon—Guidebooks. I. Title.
  GV853 .A53 2001
  796.9'2'09795—dc21
                                                    2001001903

Contents

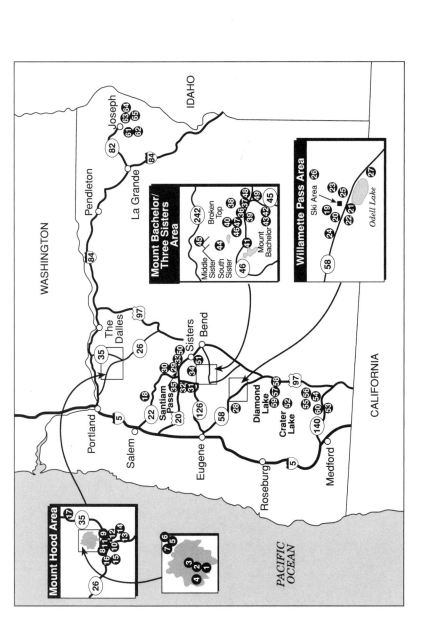

Part 5: Eastern Oregon

LEGEND

(5)	Interstate highway
(24)	U.S. highway
(36)	State highway
272	County or Forest Service road
——	Paved road or good road
══	Gravel or dirt road
-----	Trail
▲	Campground
(T)	Start of route
⌣	Bridge
⋀	Mountain peak
⌒	River or creek
▭	Lake or pond
⊥⊥⊥	Falls
→z→	North
■	Building or site
⬆	Shelter
··········	Chair lift
❄	Sno-park

Introduction

Want to know a big secret about snowshoeing? It's *easy*. Don't let anybody tell you otherwise. Snowshoes were first designed centuries ago as a utilitarian method for getting around in deep snow. They are still the simplest method of winter travel. As the saying goes, if you can walk, you can snowshoe. No special equipment, other than the shoes themselves, is required. Although your experience will improve as you practice a few techniques—some of which this book will teach you—there just isn't a lot to learn about the use of snowshoes. Anybody who is ready for winter weather is ready for a snowshoe outing. Once you've got the proper weatherproof outdoor clothing, and some basic backcountry know-how, all you need are the snowshoes themselves.

The backcountry doesn't shut down during winter. In fact, winter has the effect of reinventing the wilderness. Favorite summertime trails are reborn with winter's snowy arrival. Hikers on snowshoes can revisit a trail they explored the previous summer and find that everything has changed. Snowy robes now drape familiar trees. Lakes freeze over into silent disks of ice. Splashing streams bubble quietly under ice sculptures. The bugs—and crowds—disappear. In their place are new opportunities and new challenges.

There are as many types of snowshoeing outings as there are people who try it. For those who aren't interested in skiing, or who just want to get away from it all on a crystalline winter day, snowshoeing is the easiest and most time-efficient method for escaping civilization. Just put them on your feet and start walking. The activity lends itself to idle afternoon wanders across a snowy golf course or up a frozen river. For avid hikers who despair over the onset of winter, snowshoeing is their ticket back out into the open country. Those who set their sights higher can take snowshoes up toward the summits of the Cascade Mountains. Snowboarders who welcome the challenge of backcountry riding can trek to those slopes on top of a pair of

snowshoes. And for those who are looking for a real change of pace, snowshoeing makes the backpacking season go year-round. Winter campers may endure long, frozen nights, but they're likely to discover peace and solitude that are unavailable during the other seasons.

SNOWSHOE BASICS

As with most outdoor equipment, snowshoe styles vary, but they're all based on one simple objective: to get people above the snow by making their feet extra large. One look at a moose floating on his big feet through a snowy forest shows that snowshoes are hardly an original invention. Likewise, rabbits use their wide feet to the same advantage. Snowshoe hares can dash right across a meadow of new-fallen snow, thanks to their big feet. Wooden snowshoes have existed for centuries; in fact, some researchers list the snowshoe as one of humankind's earliest inventions. Long before horses arrived on the American continent, Indians used snowshoes when hunting buffalo on the Great Plains.

The basic design concept is fairly simple. Most snowshoes are essentially glorified tennis rackets. Their rigid outer frames, usually oval, used to be made of sturdy—but pliable—wood such as ash. In between that was the "decking" material, which was made of straps of rawhide or leather. This allowed the shoe to be light and durable but still keep a person's feet above the snow. Today most snowshoes are constructed with synthetic materials such as neoprene or Hypalon® nylon to "float" the wearer.

In the center of the decking is the binding, which used to be a mind-boggling network of laces or straps tied over and around the wearer's boots. Today's snowshoe bindings are greatly improved: some sport only a few straps; some use a series of ratcheting buckled straps; and still others work like a modern snowboarder's "step-in" binding, with a plate that snaps to a binding on the bottom of a snowboarding boot. The most common arrangement, however, consists of a few straps in critical spots: around the heel, over the instep, and across the toe. Anybody who can tie a shoe or strap on a river sandal can operate modern snowshoe bindings. A key component of the snowshoe is the toe-hole in the decking. Because the bindings are flexible, and are often only attached to a center or master cord that stretches the width of the snowshoe, there needs to be a hole for the toe to drop into while the wearer steps forward. This keeps the shoe parallel to the snow's surface without slapping up against the wearer's boots, or without shoveling snow every time the wearer takes a step.

Mount Bachelor

Snowshoer/snowboarder on Tumalo Mountain

Traditional wooden snowshoes varied in size; some of them stood as tall as their wearers. These longer models, such as the "Yukon" or "Tracker" designs, were more suited to wide-open terrain and had long wooden "tails" that functioned as a rudder, keeping the shoes oriented forward. Other snowshoes were smaller and rounder, such as the "Bearpaw," which was designed to maneuver in thick brush.

Modern snowshoes wear longer, weigh less, and are more user-friendly to beginners and experts alike. The most significant difference is the size. Newer snowshoes are basically variations on the "Western" style, invented in the 1950s, which turns out to be a versatile enough design to take anywhere. These shoes generally measure between 8 and 10 inches wide, and 25 and 40 inches long.

But the most significant design improvement is the addition of metal traction points similar to a climber's crampons. Because snowshoe routes in the Cascades can present a variety of snow conditions—from slush to hard ice—and at least one or two steep hills, having the bite of metal (or even just hard plastic points) underfoot can give a snowshoer the confidence of sure footing. Many of the older wooden snowshoes, although beautiful, lack this essential feature and might prevent a person from taking many of the trips listed in this guidebook.

One clarification, however, is necessary: even with today's safe, functional designs, snowshoes still do allow people to walk on top of all snow surfaces without sinking into the snow. Snowshoes are not magic. They are designed to displace snow, provide a platform, and keep people from "postholing" up to their hips. If you think your snowshoes aren't doing you any good because you're still sinking a few inches into the snowpack, try walking in deep snow without them. After you dig yourself back out of your hole, you will have learned a great hands-on lesson in snowshoe effectiveness.

TECHNIQUE

Learning to walk with snowshoes probably takes less time than learning how to put them on. The night before your outing, take time to figure out your snowshoe straps and adjust them for your boots. (This is *not* something you want to do in the snow at the trailhead, with your pack on and your group waiting to hit the trail.) Once you're strapped in, take a couple of steps and you'll realize it's much like walking in a pair of big boots. The only real technique you'll need to learn comes into play when you encounter hills.

Remember that your foot is now attached to a metal cleat, or crampon. When you climb a hill, use those metal spikes to your advantage and really step into the snow. Let the snowshoe's platform land on the snow normally while you focus on engaging the entire cleat. The same principle applies for descending: make sure your boot and cleat engage the snow firmly and completely. Try not to lean too far backward or

Snowshoer with baby

forward. The idea is to get as much of your foot onto the snow as possible. The platform will do its work without your forcing it.

Even the smallest and lightest snowshoes prevent you from making quick pivoting movements. Backing up is never easy because the tails of your snowshoes are likely to catch on the snow. Instead, take small circular steps to turn around. This technique will help you with steep hills. If it's too steep to climb straight up (and you need to go up, and the avalanche hazard is minimal), you can make a series of switchbacking zigzags to the top. In steep and deep snow, take longer and higher steps to keep from sliding back onto your previous step. If you use ski poles, remember not to rely on them to push yourself up the hill and off the snow. Ski poles give you balance and support, but your feet and snowshoes must do the work.

Ouch!

A WORD ABOUT ETIQUETTE

Cross-country skiers and even snowmobilers use many of the routes in this book. While proper behavior around snowmobiles consists merely of staying out of their way, there are a few considerations that snowshoers should keep in mind for good skier–snowshoer relations.

Cross-country skiers need a smooth, uninterrupted track so their ski patterns or climbing skins can have enough snow to grip. Without that, they're likely to lose traction and slip backward on hills. Nothing can harm those tracks more than a hole from a boot or snowshoe. And nothing bothers skiers more than having their smooth tracks interrupted by snowshoe holes. When sharing trails with skiers, try to make your own path and stay on it, even if you're just traveling parallel to a ski track. This will help ensure that these trails stay open to snowshoers. There's usually plenty of room out there, and it keeps everyone happy on busy trails.

WHAT YOU WILL NEED
Snowshoes
Before you decide what kind of snowshoe to use, you need to decide what kind of snowshoer you are. Factor in your weight, the weight of your pack, and the type of trips you plan to take. As a rule of thumb, the bigger you and your backpack are, the bigger your snowshoes need to be.

Most modern snowshoes are no bigger than 10 by 40 inches. If your weight with or without a pack is more than 200 pounds, you should consider getting these bigger snowshoes, even for short trips. If you weigh between 180 and 200 pounds, with or without gear, consider shoes that measure about 9 by 30 inches. Oregon's wetter snow quality, however, will allow you to get away with a smaller snowshoe in all but the lightest eastern Oregon snow. If you can buy or rent only one size of snowshoe for a variety of applications, a snowshoe of 8 by 25 inches might just do the trick. Although no snowshoe will enable you to stay completely above every kind of snow, you will maximize your efficiency by using a snowshoe properly selected for you. Rent a couple of different sizes and styles to get a feel for what you'll need. If you're like me, medium-sized but given to carrying heavy loads, a medium-sized snowshoe will work fine most of the time.

Footwear
Although you can buy "snowshoe-specific" boots, most sturdy, water-resistant hiking boots will work well for most snowshoers. For years I used an insulated "pac" boot with a rubber bottom and leather upper. This certainly kept me warm but didn't offer much support when my outings got progressively longer and more involved. Remember, this is still hiking. Wear boots that offer you both support and comfort for a long and potentially wet day. Wearing gaiters over your boots will keep snow out of your socks. Use good noncotton socks to keep your feet warm and supported. There's no good reason to ever wear a cotton sock in the backcountry because the material never dries out and offers no insulation when wet. Layering socks to ward off blisters and cold is fine as long as you don't pack your feet in too tightly. Cutting off circulation to your toes is a quick route to frostbite.

Snowshoeing in springtime

Clothing

Wool or synthetic clothing that offers insulation is really your only option for any winter outing. Again, avoid cotton clothing. Leave the tee shirt in the car, or better yet, at home.

Always pack more clothing than you need. In the Cascades, you're likely to run into a variety of temperatures during the day, and your body temperature will change as you stop, go, sweat, and stop. Develop a layering system that allows you to compensate for these changes. Next to your skin, wear a lightweight layer of long underwear, made of polypropylene, wool, silk, Capilene®, or Thermastat™. These first-layer materials wick away sweat from your skin and maintain a dry layer of insulation where it's needed most. Over the first layer, the options are limitless. Choose some kind of warm sweater, fleece coat, wool jumper, or down jacket. Down vests are excellent ways to maintain a warm core without restricting your movement. Finally, let's remember that this is Oregon. Carry a pair of waterproof/breathable pants and a jacket. A simple shell jacket compresses nicely into a backpack and will keep wind and water from infiltrating your insulation. Also, choose your accessories carefully. Consider bringing along a warm hat, gloves or mittens (the latter are warmer but offer less dexterity), and maybe even a neck gaiter.

If you're planning a strenuous trip, start off wearing just enough clothing to keep the chill off. You'll warm up soon enough. As soon as you start to sweat, it's time to remove a layer. Moisture that remains on the skin could end up freezing there, which could invite the onset of hypothermia.

Safety Equipment

As soon as the trailhead is out of site, you're in the backcountry, where you'll rely on your own preparedness to keep you safe. The Mountaineers has developed a list of Ten Essentials that everyone in your group should carry:

1. **Extra clothing.** Plan on the worst weather possible, even if the sun shines in the morning. Weather changes quickly in the mountains, and if you get injured or lost you won't be moving around much. Be ready for long periods of sitting in the cold.
2. **Extra food.** Snowshoeing is a workout, and being out in the cold requires energy. Always bring enough food so that you'll have some left over from an uneventful trip. This extra fuel will keep you warm and energized during emergencies.
3. **Sunglasses.** They're necessary in snowy conditions, where sunlight reflects off millions of snow crystals. Squinting is not enough to prevent snow blindness, a painful and debilitating condition that can create an emergency on a sunny or even a partially cloudy day.
4. **Knife.** These days, a multitool is an even better option, since the pliers that come on many of them can be used for equipment repair. You never know how useful a knife is until you don't have one.
5. **First-aid kit.** Even if you aren't trained in first aid, it's a good idea to carry enough to handle immediate problems, like cuts and sprains. Gauze bandages, pain-relief medication, and sun and burn cream are a few basics everyone should carry. A first-aid course is a good idea for anyone who plans to venture out into the backcountry.

6. **Fire starter.** A candle or other fire-starting material is the only way you'll get wet wood to burn. If you're stuck in the winter woods overnight, a campfire can keep you warm and members of your party calm.
7. **Matches.** Don't bother with anything but the windproof/waterproof variety. Lighters run out of fuel, get wet easily, and are otherwise unreliable.
8. **Flashlight.** Keep in mind that it gets dark very quickly during an Oregon winter. You may need a flashlight to find your way out after dark or to set up an emergency camp. Always carry extra batteries and bulb.
9. **Map.** First, be sure you know how to read it, and always carry the map of the area you're hiking in.
10. **Compass.** Don't carry one without knowing how to use it.

I've always carried a few other items on my trips. A snow shovel of lightweight plastic or metal is essential for safety in avalanche country and for setting up camp in the snow. I also carry a repair/emergency kit that holds a few widely applicable items: a few feet of 1-inch tubular webbing, more than a dozen feet of nylon cord, and construction-grade quick glue. Although every backpacker seems to have rolls of duct tape around, in winter switch to black electrician's tape, which sticks better in freezing temperatures. I carry a whole roll of the stuff, which can fix just about anything. A tiny mylar blanket can make a handy shelter in a pinch and takes up almost no space in your pack. A small safety mirror, sold in most backpacking shops, is great for signaling aircraft or search parties. I also carry an ace bandage for wrapping twisted ankles and knees. If you use ski poles for snowshoeing—many people find them helpful for balance or for climbing and descending steep hills—be sure to carry an extra basket. Poles are excellent tools for deep-snow trail breaking, but it's a mistake to rely on them too heavily. On a few trips in this book you'd be well advised to carry an ice ax and know how to use it.

Food and Water

Carry food that will do the job of keeping you fueled and warm. I've never left a trailhead without a few "energy bars" in my pack. They last a long time and work great as backup food. But going into the backcountry doesn't mean having to eat artificial food. Dried or fresh fruit, nuts, breads, cheeses, and a lot of water—about a quart per person every 8 hours—will keep you going on most any trip. The backcountry medicine guru Buck Tilton states that urine should be "clear and copious" in the backcountry to avoid dehydration. It may be cold and snowy, but winter air can still dehydrate the winter athlete. A tiny thermos full of hot noncaffeinated tea or broth makes a wonderful treat on winter outings. Likewise candy is nice for a treat, but sugar burns fast and won't sustain you for an extended trip.

Sno-Park Permits

Most of the snowshoe hikes in this book start at state sno-parks. Oregon's sno-park permit program provides parkings areas in all of the state's mountain passes as well as most ski, snowmobile, and snow play areas. To park in one of the sno-park areas (which are often posted with signs identifying them as "Winter Recreation Areas") between November 15 and April 30, you must have a valid sno-park permit displayed in the windshield of your vehicle. Otherwise, you may be fined.

Sno-park permits can be purchased at all Oregon Department of Motor Vehicles offices, and also from permit agents in resorts, sporting good stores, and other retail outlets. In 2001, an annual permit cost $15, a three-day permit cost $7, and a daily permit cost $3. Some permit agents may charge an additional service fee. For more information and updates on sno-park permits, call the Oregon Department of Transportation at (800) 977-ODOT (6368) or visit *www.tripcheck.com/winter/snoparks.htm.*

WINTER CAMPING

What better way to truly experience the full beauty of winter than to spend a night in the snow? The quiet of the snowy forests and mountains and the solitude and the beauty of the winter sky are great reasons for sleeping out in the wintry backcountry.

But winter camping demands more preparation and planning than summertime tenting out. Plan well in advance for your warmth, your diet, and your shelter. The consequences of not having thought out all the possibilities are more serious in the winter than they are during a warm summer night. In general you'll need more of everything: more clothing for sitting around when the temperatures are freezing; more stove fuel for making water by melting snow; a warmer sleeping bag (and a sleeping pad) for chilly nights; and a more durable tent.

When planning your itinerary, remember winter in the Pacific Northwest means short days. Unless you've been snowshoeing all winter and are accustomed to carrying heavy loads into the backcountry, you can assume that backpacking in the snow is strenuous in ways you haven't counted on. It's best to cut your day's snowshoeing short to allow for enough time to set up camp. You want to have some energy left for putting up your tent or preparing food.

Consider your camp's location carefully. Burning a fire or stove beneath a snow-laden tree can cause that snow to melt just enough to drop on your head or camp. Shelter yourself away from the wind and avalanche-prone hillsides. Remember that cold air sinks; try to avoid camping in the bottom of a deep valley. If you like, you can build a snow cave, sleep in a tent, or use some of the backcountry shelters available for public use. If you use a tent, make sure it can withstand strong gusts of wind and heavy snowfall that may build up during the night. The snow does offer you endless opportunities to practice "snow architecture." Use your snowshoes to stomp down a flat spot for your tent. For protection from wind and for more warmth, build a snow wall around your tent. You don't need more than a couple vertical feet of snow in a semicircle to do the job.

Your main goal while winter camping is to stay warm and dry. To that end, you'll need a serious sleeping bag designed for cold temperatures. Modern synthetic bags are cheaper, lightweight, and warm. Of course, nothing beats a down-filled sleeping bag for warmth and low weight. Down bags cost more, however, and the trick with down is keeping it dry; it doesn't insulate much at all if it's wet. Besides a warm sleeping bag, you'll want warm, dry clothes. I like to change into dry clothes as soon as I get to camp; that way I'm ready to tackle other projects such as preparing food and shelter. If you do have wet items that you'll want for the next day, the only way to really dry them out is to drag the soggy things into your sleeping bag. Few things are less appealing on a cold winter night than sleeping with a pair of soggy socks, but you decide just how badly you'll want dry gear on the next cold morning. Finally, if the temperatures are well below freezing, sleep with your water bottle to keep it from freezing. To make this last task more inviting, fill your bottle with warm (not boiling) water before you go to bed. A good old hot water bottle is one of the oldest tricks in the book for warding off the chills on a winter night.

AVALANCHE SAFETY

This guide is not a replacement for essential avalanche safety courses, books, or videos. Anyone going into hilly territory is headed into avalanche country. Unfortunately, avalanches occur because of processes that are difficult to gauge just by looking at a pristine hillside. Here's one rule of thumb that has never failed any backcountry traveler: *if it looks like it could slide, then it probably will.* Maybe not today, maybe not tomorrow, but you can't be sure. This rule is annoyingly simplistic, but it's a useful thing to remember when you begin second-guessing avalanche terrain.

The best way to avoid avalanche hazard is to use your senses. Snow that is poorly bonded beneath the surface will most likely release and start an avalanche. Watch the weather. Dramatic changes in temperature or

Doing an avalanche pit test

weather patterns can affect the stability of the snow. Avalanches occur most frequently on slope angles between 30 and 45 degrees, but they have been known to occur on angles as shallow as 25 degrees or as steep as 70 degrees. Also look at the terrain in front of you. Avalanches are much more likely to occur on convex slopes with a bulge in the middle, or on concave slopes with a steep upper section. Look at the vegetation. Are the trees sparse in one gully and not in another? If so, it may mean that avalanches have scoured the area before. If it's warm out, well above freezing, watch for gloppy snow that sticks to your snowshoes and boots. This sort of wet snow can also slide easily because water is melting down through the snowpack and weakening its structural integrity.

Besides using your senses, you should check all available information. Several avalanche hot lines cover portions of Oregon, and many local forest service or park service offices maintain avalanche and snow condition hot lines. They are listed at the top of the hike descriptions, where applicable. The National Oceanic and Atmospheric Administration's weather forecasts (available through a special weather radio or the agency's website, *www.nws.noaa.gov*) can tell backcountry travelers a lot about the sort of snow and weather conditions that await them. The National Avalanche Center's website, *www.nwn.noaa.gov/sites/nwac,* provides a detailed synopsis of weather and snow conditions. This extensive site covers most of the Cascade mountain region. Also, be sure to call the Oregon Avalanche Report (which covers Mount Hood and the southern Cascades) at (503) 326-2400.

USING THIS BOOK

The hikes listed in this guide are designed to inspire your own adventures, fire your imagination, and show you a good representation of the opportunities in Oregon's winter landscape. It should not replace individual planning and ideas. Use your summer hiking guides as further inspiration for good snowshoeing routes. In this book, the route descriptions are designed to help you plan your hike, but they are not the last word on each route. That comes from you after you've completed a trip and found the best routes, methods, and tools for the job.

To guarantee that your initial snowshoeing experience is positive, start with an easy route. As simple as it may become, your first experience with snowshoeing will necessarily require several adjustments. You'll have to get a group together, find a route to tackle, get the shoes sized up properly, pack the right clothes, prepare enough food and water, and check the weather and avalanche notices. In Oregon, the winters are long and usually very snowy; you can count on a lot of time to tackle more ambitious trips later.

Understanding the Chapter Information

Each route starts with essential, at-a-glance information to make it easy for you to decide if the hike is right for you and your group.

Trail Ratings. The hike ratings in this book are subjective, and not everyone will agree with every rating. Keep this in mind as you select routes. The ratings are based on the following guidelines:

Easy: No previous snowshoeing experience is required. These trails are great for a first attempt or for families. Elevation gain or loss, routefinding, and avalanche challenges are all minimal on these hikes.

More difficult: You will need more experience with snowshoes because of the climbing and descending on these routes. Also, because of moderate avalanche danger, many of these trails will require more planning. Length alone can designate a trail as "more difficult."

Most difficult: Avalanche hazard needs to be considered on every one of these trips. The routes reach significant heights, and proficiency with snowshoes on steep traverses, climbs, or descents is required. You may need to carry and know how to use an ice ax for self-arrest.

Backcountry: Often a trail gets a "backcountry" rating because there are no obvious trails or roads to follow, and hikers will need to be skilled with map and compass to complete them. You need solid avalanche awareness, mountaineering, and winter survival skills to safely complete many of these trips.

Round Trip. This estimation varies only because starting points will change depending on where snowpack ends on certain access roads and parking areas. A trip that was 5 miles in a low snow year could double if the road leading to the trailhead is snowed out. Trips that start and end in developed sno-parks will contain the most consistent estimations.

Starting Elevation. This number is an estimation, as snow levels can change the starting point of the hike.

High Point. This number represents the highest elevation point, not necessarily the ending point.

Best Hiking Time. This is a "best guess" based on an average snow year. I've done my best to offer a window of time within which you will encounter sufficient snow and decent weather to carry out the trip. But the Cascade Mountains have a way of confounding attempts to categorize an "average" snow year. A deep, stable snowpack creates the best snowshoeing

Water Tower Trail

conditions. It would be nice if the weather were calm and clear. It would be even nicer if the avalanche danger were negligible. However, it's a rare day when all of these factors coincide. Use this category as a good indicator and be prepared to make your own decisions based on information gathered from forest rangers, weather forecasters, or others who have recently traveled the trails.

Maps. The maps included in this book aren't intended for wilderness navigation. They should help you locate trailheads and significant landmarks. They are in no way intended as replacements for good topographic maps and a compass. You'll quickly find that navigating in the winter is a lot different than in summer; for one thing, the trail is rarely visible, and neither are some trail markers.

Where possible, I've listed commercially produced maps that overlap maps produced by the United States Geological Survey (USGS) and the United States Forest Service (USFS). Often these privately produced maps (such as the Geo-Graphics and Green Trails maps) are more helpful than the USGS or USFS maps; the information is more recent, and trail distances and features are clearly marked. Most larger outdoor equipment stores stock the Geo-Graphics maps and a few others stock the Green Trails maps, which are listed by number in a grid.

Who to Contact. Start every trip with a call to the Oregon Avalanche Report, which covers Mount Hood and the southern Cascades, at (503) 326-2400. Most of the numbers listed with each hike are for U.S. Forest Service ranger district offices. These offices maintain information on road conditions and trail usage, and some may have staff available to answer more complicated questions about avalanche hazards and trail conditions.

A NOTE ABOUT SAFETY

Safety is an important concern in all outdoor activities. No guidebook can alert you to every hazard or anticipate the limitations of every reader. Therefore, the descriptions of roads, trails, routes, and natural features in this book are not representations that a particular place or excursion will be safe for your party. When you follow any of the routes described in this book, you assume responsibility for your own safety. Under normal conditions, such excursions require the usual attention to traffic, road and trail conditions, weather, terrain, the capabilities of your party, and other factors. Keeping informed on current conditions and exercising common sense are the keys to a safe, enjoyable outing.

The Mountaineers Books

Northeast face of Mount Hood

PART 1

Near Portland

--1--

Silcox Hut

Rating: More difficult
Round trip: 2 miles
Starting elevation: 5,000 feet
High point: 6,920 feet at Silcox Hut
Best season: January through June
Maps: USFS Mount Hood Wilderness; Green Trails No. 462, Mount Hood; USGS Mount Hood South
Who to contact: Mount Hood National Forest, Zigzag Ranger Station, (541) 662-3191

If you're lucky, you can stretch the snowshoeing season and do this easy trip well into early summer. The glaciers above Timberline Lodge stick around so long that ski racers use the Palmer Snowfield as a year-round training area. Tucked in below the hubbub of the Palmer chair lift is this gem of Oregon history; the Silcox Hut represents some of Oregon's mountaineering glory days, as well as its philanthropic future. The old Silcox Hut was originally built in 1939 as a warming hut for mountaineers, and it still serves that purpose admirably. The sturdy construction of rock and massive Oregon timbers was designed to withstand the foul weather that frequently slams the mountain. The cabin had fallen into disrepair, but in the 1980s a coalition of climbers, historic preservationists, and architects "rescued" it. After the renovation project the Silcox Hut has a new lease on life as a combination warming cabin, café (in season), and overnight destination. It's even been used in a comedy short by Portland filmmaker Steve Sandoz; the cabin was a stand-in for a monastery.

The Silcox Hut makes for a great short day trip in good weather. Getting to Silcox Hut takes a bit of work, since you'll be climbing a mile up the mountain, well above tree line. That means that even though the distance is short, all the rules of high-mountain backcountry travel should apply. Mount Hood is notorious for attracting "sneaker" storms that appear out of nowhere. During whiteout conditions it's frighteningly easy to lose your way on the glaciers. If you think you might go beyond Silcox onto the mountain's higher slopes, you should sign in at the climbers' registry, located within the newer portion of Timberline Ski Area's Wy'East Day Lodge. The registry is available 24 hours a day, 7 days a week.

To get to Timberline Lodge, take Highway 26 east from Portland to

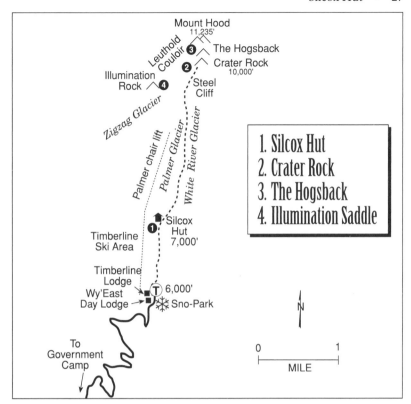

Mount Hood
11,235'

The Hogsback

Crater Rock
10,000'

Leuthold Couloir

Illumination Rock

Steel Cliff

Zigzag Glacier

Palmer chair lift

Palmer Glacier

White River Glacier

1. Silcox Hut
2. Crater Rock
3. The Hogsback
4. Illumination Saddle

Silcox Hut
7,000'

Timberline Ski Area

Timberline Lodge

Wy'East Day Lodge

6,000'

Sno-Park

To Government Camp

N

0   1
MILE

Government Camp; the turnoff toward Timberline Lodge is barely a mile past the eastern edge of town. To get to Silcox, head for the climber's trail just north of the lower Timberline parking lot. Travel just to the east of the groomed ski trails. It's a good idea to stay off the groomed area for a few reasons. For one, if you travel the groomers you'll be in the way of speeding skiers and snowboarders. Second, you may block the path of snow cats as they ply the mountain's slopes. If you're hiking in a whiteout or early in the morning, snow cat drivers can't see you until they're almost right on top of you.

The Silcox Hut is just a mile up the mountain. If you wander too far to the east on your way up, you may step onto the White River Glacier, which can drop sharply away. If you stay on the well-traveled main trail, you'll hit Silcox within an hour. If the weather makes it difficult to navigate but you're still bent on getting to Silcox, try an alternative way to get there. From the old Timberline Lodge, follow the chair lift line up the mountain. When this chair lift ends, go east toward the base of the uppermost chair lift. Due east of the base of the top-most chair lift is the Silcox Hut. Most seasons there is a cat track leading almost to the door of Silcox.

Once at Silcox, drop your pack and stack your snowshoes on the porch. If the weather's good, there will be picnic tables arranged out front. If the weather's lousy, head into the cabin's cozy interior and soak in the atmosphere. The café hours vary, but you should be able to purchase food and drinks on the days someone is staffing the counter. I've never seen them begrudge a thirsty climber a glass of water.

--2--
Crater Rock

Rating: Backcountry
Round trip: 2 miles to Silcox Hut; 6 miles to Crater Rock
Starting elevation: Approximately 6,000 feet
High point: 7,000 feet at Silcox Hut; 10,000 feet at Crater Rock
Best season: January through June
Maps: USFS Mount Hood Wilderness; Green Trails No. 462, Mount Hood; USGS Mount Hood South
Who to contact: Mount Hood National Forest, Zigzag Ranger Station, (541) 662-3191

Here's a good challenge for those who want to take their snowshoes into the alpine zone of Mount Hood, Oregon's highest peak. Although going farther up toward the summit of Mount Hood would require technical climbing equipment and know-how, this trip gets you well above the clouds and offers a view unlike few others in the state. On a spring day when clouds and fog blanket the city of Portland, hikers at Crater Rock are often basking in sunshine. Make no mistake, however; this is a strenuous trip with significant elevation gain. To manage the steep angle of the slopes below Crater Rock, allow at least six hours for the hike, bring an ice ax, and be prepared to self-arrest should you slip. Avalanche hazard can be considerable on some of the higher slopes. On this route your group also can split up and allow some members to stop hiking at the old Silcox Hut, which is just 1,000 feet above your starting elevation (most shoers can get there in about 2 hours). This historic cabin, built in 1939 as a warming hut for the old Magic Mile chair lift, has been reborn as a café, inn, and climbers' shelter. (It's also a great place to cool your heels on a sunny mountain day.) Take note, however, that the Silcox Hut is barely one-third of the way to

View from Crater Rock

Crater Rock, which is far above in the rugged alpine zone of Mount Hood. From Silcox Hut you will need to be on your toes: avalanche hazard, weather exposure, and the chances of getting lost all increase as you ascend.

These hikes begin at Timberline Lodge, another historic site. To get there from Portland, turn off Highway 26 at Government Camp and take the Timberline Mountain Road 6 miles up to the ski lodge parking lot. The climbers' trailhead is clearly marked. Before you go anywhere, be sure you sign in at the climbers' registry at the Wy'East Day Lodge. The registry is accessible 24 hours a day, 7 days a week. Even though you're not climbing the entire mountain, you're still entering an area with some moderate avalanche danger and potentially low visibility in poor weather. It's also easy to lose your way descending the mountain in low visibility; coming straight down the fall line would take you directly into either Zigzag or White River Canyons. Once in those canyons, avalanche danger increases exponentially and neither of them returns you to Timberline Lodge. Of course, this is only really a hazard in low visibility. The proper routes are easy to locate in better weather, not least because you share the mountain with climbers and skiers who flock to the area. Timberline is famous for its year-round snowfields that allow ski racers to train in the middle of summer. And the summit itself is one of the most-climbed peaks in North America.

As you ascend, travel just to the right, or east, of the groomed ski trails on the Palmer Glacier. Be sure to avoid the snow cats as they groom the slopes in the early morning hours; snow cat drivers are not in the habit of watching for climbers or snowshoers and don't take kindly to people messing up their work. You can use the Palmer chair lift to gauge your upward progress. The chair lift tops out at around 8,500 feet. On a clear day, Crater Rock is visible as a prominent rock outcropping that juts skyward off the south side of Mount Hood's summit. At its base you can perch for a snack or, weather permitting, a lunch break. Prepared climbers with ice axes and crampons will go farther on up The Hogsback, heading up the steep and exposed ridge toward the 11,235-foot summit.

Start in the early morning to take advantage of limited winter light and solid snow in the late spring months. By the time June rolls around, you're likely to encounter soft, slushy snow after 9 or 10 in the morning, which can increase the avalanche hazard dramatically. Use caution and exercise prudent planning.

--ʒ--
The Hogsback

Rating: Backcountry
Round trip: 6 miles
Starting elevation: Approximately 6,000 feet
High point: 10,000 feet
Best season: January through August
Maps: USFS Mount Hood Wilderness; Green Trails No. 462, Mount Hood; USGS Mount Hood South
Who to contact: Mount Hood National Forest, Zigzag Ranger Station, (541) 662-3191

There isn't a big difference between this route and the Crater Rock route (Route 2), save for the extra push toward the saddle that forms The Hogsback on Mount Hood. You're gaining a little better view, a little better thigh burn, and a little more exposure on the mountain's uppermost reaches.

You're also going to get exposed to some major sulfur up here; this route passes by huge open fumaroles, which serve as excellent reminders of Mount Hood's true identity as a volcano. You might suspect horrible things of your hiking partner before you realize that the smell is from the sulfur, which comes steaming out of the great open surface vents. Geologists characterize fumarole activity as a sign of a volcano's age. Although some might wish to see Mount Hood blow its top in their lifetime, it's more likely that these fumaroles are about as dramatic as Mount Hood will get.

The Hogsback is also the last staging point for climbers headed up the final pitch toward the summit of Mount Hood. By the time most climbers get to The Hogsback, they're pretty whipped from hauling safety gear, ropes, crampons, and ice axes all the way up the mountain. The south-side route, which you're essentially following to get to The Hogsback, is also the most popular route for weekend warriors looking for an easy summit to climb. Therefore you're likely to see all stripes of climbers on this route, from seasoned alpinists moving fast and light to worn-out newcomers wearing old blue jeans and struggling for the summit above.

Your delight, then, is in skipping the climbing burden altogether and taking in the view from this hard-won bench high up on the flanks of Mount Hood. The skiers at the Timberline Ski Area, if they're visible, look like tiny ants. The finest moment on The Hogsback comes during the late spring or early summer, when climbers and snowshoers sit in the sunshine above cloud layers that have Portland fully socked in.

Getting to The Hogsback means following directions to Timberline Lodge. From Portland take Highway 26 east to Government Camp. The turnoff toward Timberline is on your left, just a mile past the eastern edge of town. Be sure to register at the Wy'East Day Lodge, even if you don't

The Hogsback

plan on summitting Mount Hood. You're still entering terrain that is given to avalanches, foul weather, and sheer icy slopes. Follow the climber's trail from the Timberline Lodge parking area. Along the way pass Silcox Hut and Crater Rock. It's a substantial bit of vertical gain to get to The Hogsback, so be prepared for a workout. The Hogsback is just north of Crater Rock and up the slope above the fumaroles.

Crevasses aren't an issue for this route, but, as you're sitting on The Hogsback, take note of the massive bergschrund, or large crevasse, up above you on the steep slopes toward the summit. If you watch climbers head for the top, you'll see that this famous feature of Mount Hood is a daunting obstacle. Snowshoe crampons may help you climb up to The Hogsback, but you'll quickly see that much more substantial tools are needed for a summit attempt.

--4--
Illumination Saddle

Rating: Backcountry
Round trip: 5 miles
Starting elevation: 5,800 feet
High point: 9,500 feet
Best season: December through August
Maps: USFS Mount Hood Wilderness; Green Trails No. 462, Mount Hood; USGS Mount Hood South
Who to contact: Mount Hood National Forest, Zigzag Ranger Station, (541) 662-3191

There's nothing like telling your friends you're off to go snowshoeing in the middle of July. On this route that's entirely possible, and in fact isn't a bad time to go. You're virtually guaranteed good weather and, if you get up early enough, good snow. Despite the ever-present challenges of Mount Hood's upper reaches, this is nonetheless a great shorter hike that gets you into some amazing terrain. It's just enough off the beaten path of the climber's trail to the summit of Mount Hood that you'll get a little peace and quiet, and Illumination Saddle is every bit as dramatic as any other part of the mountain. More than a few picture calendars boast photographs of this scenic spot, and when you get there you'll see why. It's a stunning alpine perch.

That said, you will begin this hike just like Routes 1, 2, and 3. From

Portland drive east on Highway 26 until you reach Government Camp. On your way east out of town, notice a signed turnoff for Timberline Lodge. Follow the winding road up to the lodge. Once you reach Timberline Lodge be sure to sign in at the climbers' registry. Again, it doesn't matter if it's July 4 and you're wearing shorts with your snowshoes. This is still the mountain that changes weather in five minutes if it is so inclined, and you'd do well to follow the usual alpine backcountry precautions. In fact, in sunny spring weather you can witness (or participate in, if you're unlucky) a wet spring avalanche, where snow gets so saturated with water from the melting process that upper layers just wash away down the mountain. The flanks of Illumination Rock (which is the landmark you'll aim for) are steep enough for a spring avalanche, so be wary.

Illumination Rock is located to the west of the traditional climber's route, well above the upper end of the Palmer Snowfield, where ski racers and snowboarders train in the summer months. It's also at the lower end of the Leuthold Couloir, a steep pitch that leads to the summit of Mount Hood. That means if you like you can follow the chair lift lines up toward Illumination Rock and its adjacent saddle. Avoid this area during daylight hours, however, when flying skiers and snowboarders dominate the snowfields. Another option is to follow the climber's trail. When you get to the top of the groomed snowfield, Illumination Rock and Illumination Saddle will be to the northwest, or to climber's left. The chair lift tops out at about 8,400 feet, so at this point you'll know you're within 1,000 feet of your destination.

The saddle, which is just uphill from the sides of Illumination Rock, is a great place to drop your pack and eat lunch or breakfast. It's also just wide enough to pitch a climber's tent, and you just might encounter that here. Even if there's a tent on the saddle, there's still room for a couple of lunching snowshoers, so head on up anyway. You won't want to miss the vantage point from the saddle: you can look north into the Reid Glacier and the west side of Mount Hood, or across the slope you can see struggling alpinists trudging up the climber's route to the summit.

In poor visibility this route can get you into trouble because of the open quality of upper Mount Hood. Keep that in mind as you head back down. Going directly down the fall line will take you into the upper reaches of Zigzag Canyon and Zigzag Glacier, two places you don't want to be unless you're hoping to practice your crevasse rescue techniques. In all seriousness, be prepared: in case you get blinded by a sudden storm or even fog, be sure you can follow a map and compass back to the safety of the Palmer Snowfield.

--*5*--

Cloud Cap Inn

Rating: More difficult
Round trip: 3.5 miles one way; 12-mile loop along Cloud Cap Road
Starting elevation: 3,900 feet
High point: 5,920 feet at Cloud Cap Inn
Best season: November through April
Maps: USFS Mount Hood Wilderness; Green Trails No. 462, Mount Hood; Mark Wigg, Mount Hood Ski Trails
Who to contact: Mount Hood National Forest, Hood River Ranger District, (541) 352-6002

If you take the Tilly Jane Trail to the Cloud Cap Inn, you'll encounter about 100 yards of relatively flat terrain on this trip—and that's in the parking lot. Otherwise plan on a lot of uphill on the trip to this historic cabin—and allow at least 4 to 8 hours to do the trip. Don't attempt it without a sturdy set of calf muscles. Also plan on jaw-dropping views of Mount Hood.

View of Mount Hood from Cloud Cap

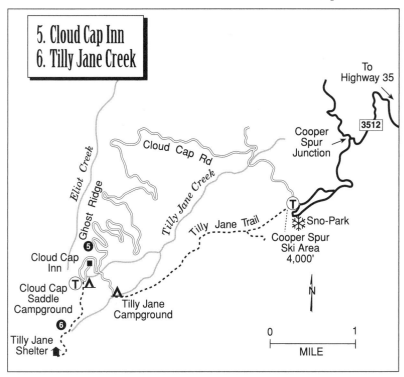

5. Cloud Cap Inn
6. Tilly Jane Creek

Cloud Cap Inn itself offers a slice of Oregon mountaineering history. The old cabin was originally built in 1889 as a resort for wealthy tourists who would take a horse-drawn wagon to the cabin. Today the cabin is the headquarters for the Hood River–based Crag Rats alpine club, which operates as a mountain rescue group when needed. From their porch, Crag Rat members sometimes set up a telescope to monitor climbers' progress on the east face of Mount Hood, which towers over the cabin. Just across the snowed-covered parking lot is the Snowshoe Club cabin, another historical structure. This 100-year-old clubhouse is the year-round home to a Portland-based private outing club. Neither cabin is open to the public, but their sturdy exteriors offer testimony to the challenge of maintaining an ancient wooden structure at tree line.

The trip starts at the Cooper Spur Sno-Park, which is next to the Cooper Spur Ski Area, a tiny hill popular with local families. From Portland, take Highway 26 east toward Government Camp on Mount Hood. Cooper Spur is about 20 miles beyond Government Camp. Turn off on paved Forest Road 3511, then in a few miles turn left on Forest Road 3512 to reach the Cooper Spur junction. The sno-park is less than 4 miles up the road from the junction. Park by the snow gate to the Cloud Cap Road and find the Tilly Jane Trail just a few steps away from the parking lot. From here it's all uphill on a long ridge. Watch out for descending skiers who may be out of control on this steep trail.

In 3 miles of grueling uphill, just before you cross a steep ravine, you'll hit the Tilly Jane Campground and pass a couple of public overnight shelters. If you plan to sleep here, contact the Forest Service Hood River Ranger District office to make reservations a few weeks prior to any trip. Because the terrain above Cloud Cap is excellent for skiing, climbing, and sightseeing, these cabins are popular and likely to be crowded, especially on winter weekends.

Once across the ravine, you'll hit the Cloud Cap Road in a few hundred yards. Walk another 100 yards on the roadbed, but when the road turns right, you should turn left and make the final grunt through a meadow to the Cloud Cap parking area. Take a lunch break at one of several spots around the Cloud Cap Inn and enjoy a stunning view of Mount Hood's craggy east face.

For the return trip, choose one of two routes. Those who are looking for a break for tired calf muscles can take the 8.5-mile Cloud Cap Road back to the parking lot. It's a long but gentle grade all the way. If you've got the moxie for a knee-punishing run down the Tilly Jane Trail, you will get back sooner but see less of the Mount Hood backcountry. Many of the road's upper switchbacks offer views of Mount Hood and the steep canyon of Eliot Creek. There is also a third unmarked route down, on Ghost Ridge. You can follow this ridge above Eliot

Snowshoeing at Cloud Cap

Creek and bypass some of the road's twists and turns, but come prepared for backcountry navigation. Take it from one who's been there: it's easy to miss the road's switchbacks and wander aimlessly in the woods of Mount Hood.

--6--
Tilly Jane Creek

Rating:	Easy
Round trip:	3 miles
Starting elevation:	5,920 feet at Cloud Cap Inn
High point:	6,600 feet
Best season:	January through March
Maps:	USFS Mount Hood Wilderness; Green Trails No. 462, Mount Hood; Mark Wigg, Mount Hood Ski Trails
Who to contact:	Mount Hood National Forest, Hood River Ranger District, (541) 352-6002

Tilly Jane was the jaunty nickname of Mrs. William Ladd of Portland. The Ladds made many trips to this area, often staying at the Cloud Cap Inn, where this hike starts. Mr. Ladd himself was partially responsible for the construction of Cloud Cap Inn in 1889, along with C. E. S. Wood, also of Portland. A glacier on the northwest slope of Mount Hood, west of Pulpit Rock, was named after Mr. Ladd.

Mrs. Ladd must have been a delightful woman, for this creek is lovely in all seasons. Although it might be hidden beneath snow during the winter, you can still hear it burbling beneath the white stuff.

To take this great little trip, you first have to get to Cloud Cap Inn. Because the road into the Cloud Cap area is gated and closed all winter, you will need to park at the Cooper Spur Sno-Park and snowshoe your way to Cloud Cap (see Route 5). After you've spent the night at a forest service shelter or just pitched a tent in the area, Tilly Jane makes for a great half-day destination with a lot of potential for side explorations.

Start at the Cloud Cap Saddle Campground, which is just down the road from the Cloud Cap Inn. At the south end of the campground you should be able to find a forest service sign indicating the boundary of the Mount Hood Wilderness. From here travel due south along the base of a steep hillside.

After about a mile of this you'll empty out into a small alpine canyon in perfect V shape. This is the canyon of Tilly Jane Creek, and even in its depths you can get a good look at Mount Hood's north side. In the summer this canyon is filled with alpine wildflowers; in the winter it's a gently sloping pocket of winter.

Continue south up-canyon for a half mile and you'll reach the Tilly Jane Shelter. This is a good place to stop and then return the way you came. Going farther south will take you above timberline toward Cooper Spur (see Route 7), and map and compass skills will be essential once you climb free of the trees.

--⁊--
Cooper Spur

Rating: Most difficult/backcountry
Round trip: 4 miles from Cloud Cap Inn
Starting elevation: 5,900 feet at Cloud Cap Inn
High point: 8,500 feet at Cooper Spur
Best season: December through May
Maps: USFS Mount Hood Wilderness; Green Trails No. 462, Mount Hood; Mark Wigg, Mount Hood Ski Trails
Who to contact: Mount Hood National Forest, Hood River Ranger District, (541) 352-6002

Here's another trip on Mount Hood's east side that can either be a grueling push from freezing level or an exhilarating jaunt from a camp at Cloud Cap. You will travel way into the alpine backcountry of Mount Hood here. From the top of Cooper Spur, the flanks of Mount Hood look steep. But I've been on several trips to "the Spur" and invariably someone will declare that it looks like a "hop, skip, and a jump" to the summit from there. In reality, you're 2,700 feet and many terrifying rope lengths from the summit. Best to admire it from the relative safety of Cooper Spur.

Cooper Spur was named for an outdoorsman and early settler in the Hood River valley. David Rose Cooper apparently enjoyed camping not far from this scenic spot in the late nineteenth century, and you'll see why. The spot is majestic and inspiring for weekend mountaineers of all stripes. It's also a popular place for backcountry skiers and snowshoers; if you see fellow snowshoers marching up the same trail from the Cooper Spur Sno-Park with snowboards strapped to their backs, you can just about guaran-

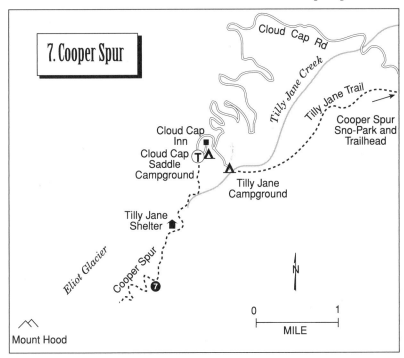

tee they're headed for this spot. The wide open slopes below Cooper Spur have an even angle that backcountry glisse connoisseurs live for.

Cooper Spur is a handy dividing line between the crevasse-ridden Eliot Glacier to the north and west, and the Newton Clark Glacier to the south. Even in this relatively mellow terrain you're still exposed to everything Old Man Winter can toss at you, including the usual winter backcountry hazards of avalanche and even some crevasses. Carry an altimeter if you have one and try to stay below 8,500 feet. Going higher than that puts you in well-documented crevasse territory.

In addition, there are no defined trails even though the area sees more activity than other sides of Mount Hood. Although many backcountry skiers or riders frequent the area, *do not* simply follow their tracks uphill. Carry a map to avoid getting drawn off-course by the tracks of someone looking not for Cooper Spur proper, but powder snow to descend. Also, timberline here is about 6,000 feet, meaning that you may not even see your own tracks on the way back down, because they may have been filled in by driving wind or snow.

Its danger aside, Cooper Spur is magnificent country. Mount Hood is

Snowshoer in the Mount Hood area

a wildly undulating mass of glaciers and moraines here, and its summit looms so dramatically above you that you are reminded of just why it's so visible from around the state.

To get there from Portland, take Interstate 84 east to Hood River, then go south on Highway 35. The turnoff onto paved Forest Road 3511 is about 20 miles from Hood River. Follow this road for a few miles and then turn left onto Forest Road 3512 to reach the Cooper Spur junction. The trailhead is just 4 miles up the road at the Cooper Spur Sno-Park. From there you need to snowshoe 3.5 miles up the Tilly Jane Trail to the Tilly Jane Campground (see Route 5).

You can go two ways from the Tilly Jane Campground to Cooper Spur. One way is to follow Tilly Jane Creek from the campground and the Tilly Jane Shelter, to just about timberline, where the drainage becomes less distinct. At that point you will follow what should be a relatively distinct ridgeline to the southwest. On a clear day you can see how this prominent ridge forms a buttress line straight toward the mountaintop. On a classic Oregon winter day (read: cloudy and snowy), pack a map and compass. Again, an altimeter is very handy on this route.

There's an old stone climber's shelter at 6,600 feet on the Cooper Spur ridge. There's nothing much in there other than shelter from the elements and some pack rats who delight in sharing your food, whether you're willing or not. You may see climbers' overnight packs stashed here while their owners tackle the summit.

The other way to Cooper Spur and this shelter is to turn away from Tilly Jane Creek at the Tilly Jane Campground. Head uphill and cross a steep ravine. In a few hundred yards you'll reach the Cloud Cap Road. Follow the road for a hundred yards more, but when the road turns right you need to turn left. Cross the meadow to reach the Cloud Cap parking area. Head to the Cloud Cap Saddle Campground, just down the road from the Cloud Cap Inn. At the south end of the campground you should see a Forest Service sign indicating the boundary of the Mount Hood Wilderness. From here travel due south along the base of a steep hillside. After about a mile of this you'll find yourself in the Tilly Jane Creek canyon, which leads to the Tilly Jane Shelter. From there follow the directions to Cooper Spur above.

Avoid traveling directly on the ridge itself. Instead, it's safer and easier to climb in the wide snowfields and valleys just east of the ridge. That way you're less exposed to the weather, and your chances of slipping and falling down the steep moraine's sides and into Eliot Glacier are reduced. In the summertime the trail to Cooper Spur does just that, zigzagging up through the remaining snowfields and scrawny mountain meadows to the spur.

There aren't a lot of signals to tell you you've arrived at Cooper Spur, but you'll see the ridge climbing sharply in angle and elevation toward the summit, and that's where you should stop. Going farther requires mountaineering equipment and know-how.

--8--
Crosstown Trail

Rating: Easy
Round trip: 3 miles
Starting elevation: 3,600 feet
High point: 4,200 feet
Best season: December through February
Maps: USGS Government Camp; Green Trails No. 461, Government Camp; Mark Wigg, Mount Hood Ski Trails
Who to contact: Mount Hood National Forest, Zigzag Ranger District, (541) 622-3191

Take this great short trail if the weather is inclement or if you've got friends headed to the Multorpor Ski Area but you'd rather be out on your webs.

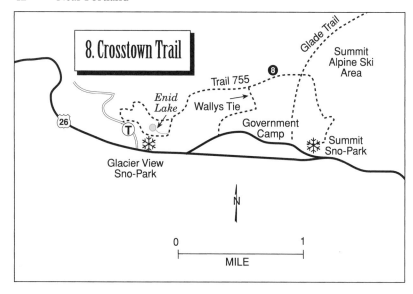

It's short enough that you'll get a good snowshoeing outing under your belt without much fuss, and, because the trail sneaks through the very edge of the town of Government Camp, you can bail out of the route at several points. In fact, at one point during this hike you'll be just a few dozen yards away from a hotel and several other "Govie" Camp properties.

Despite its proximity to the bustling little ski town, the Crosstown Trail, sometimes called the "Camptown" Trail, is a great short hike with a lot of options. You'll end up traveling from one end of Government Camp to the other by the time you've completed this hike, so remember to arrange a shuttle. You can leave one car at the tiny Summit Alpine Ski Area at the Summit and Mazama Sno-Parks, and start from the Glacier View Sno-Park on the western end of the loop (that's the way most folks do the trip). The Glacier View Sno-Park is about 1 mile away from the edge of "Govie." If you choose not to shuttle, walk back through the woods. Not only is it more scenic than just walking through town, but also Highway 26 in the winter is too dangerous for walking, even if it's only for a mile just to get back to your car.

To access the trailhead for the Crosstown Trail, take Highway 26 east from Portland; from Hood River, take the Highway 35 exit out of the Columbia River Gorge and then head southwest on Highway 26. Because Govie is practically equidistant from Portland using either route, it doesn't much matter which way you go. The Glacier View Sno-Park is located just a mile west of Government Camp off Highway 26, on the north side of the high-way. In fact, it's less than a mile east of the Mirror Lake Sno-Park on the south side of the road.

The same trailhead is used to get to Enid Lake; there is, in fact, a short loop—about 1.2 miles—that circles this little lake. Choose this loop trail if you find the weather turning worse or if your own plans change. To find the Enid Lake loop, walk north from the end of the plowed road to take the second right-hand trail. The first right is the quick access to the Crosstown Trail. That said, you could still do the Enid Loop and turn east when you get onto Trail 755, which is the forest service's number for the Crosstown Trail.

The Crosstown Trail climbs gently to the east and gains less than 1,000 feet toward the Summit Alpine Ski Area. It's a nice mixed forest dominated by subalpine elevation fir trees. There's even a quick trail out of the woods, called Wallys Tie, which leads you back to town in a mile. Continue straight on the Crosstown Trail to reach the Summit Sno-Park. Within 2 miles you'll cross the Glade Trail, which is also a getaway trail from the Timberline Ski Area up the mountain. Keep an eye out for skiers speeding down from that area to Government Camp. Again, you can opt to take the Glade Trail down and back to town, but if you cross the trail you'll finish up the Crosstown Trail and get to the upper end of an old access road. The trail drops out of the woods here toward the Summit Sno-Park and back into the bustle of Government Camp.

--9--
White River

Rating:	More difficult
Round trip:	3 miles
Starting elevation:	4,200 feet
High point:	4,800 feet
Best season:	December through March
Maps:	Green Trails No. 462, Mount Hood; USGS Mount Hood South; USFS Mount Hood National Forest
Who to contact:	Mount Hood National Forest, Bear Springs Work Center, (541) 467-2291

There are good reasons why this area is so popular. For starters, from the moment you get out of your car the view of Mount Hood is spectacular,

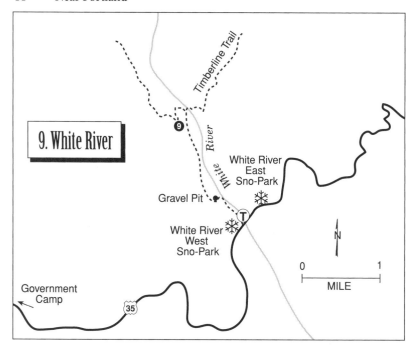

9. White River

Timberline Trail

White River East Sno-Park

Gravel Pit

White River West Sno-Park

White River

White River

Government Camp

35

N

0   1
MILE

and it just keeps getting better. It's well worth the extra weight in your pack to carry a camera, because you'll be facing Oregon's biggest peak squarely for almost the entire route. The White River Sno-Park is also uniquely positioned to give you access to several winter playgrounds on the south side of Mount Hood.

The trail from the parking lot is heavily used on weekends and holidays. But if you keep on walking, you should notice that the traffic fades significantly after about a half mile.

The White River is appropriately named in either season. In the summer it runs frothy with rapids and sediments from the uphill glaciers. In the winter your only clue to its presence will be occasional under-foot gurglings. Don't be fooled, however: if you choose to cross the waterway, be sure that you're on a solid snow bridge.

Getting to the White River Sno-Park involves a short drive east from Government Camp. From Portland take Highway 26 southeast to Government Camp; in 2 more miles take the Hood River exit, which will put you onto Highway 35. Follow this road north for just over 4 miles to the White River Sno-Park. There are actually two parking lots; park in the western one. If you cross the actual waterway, you've gone too far.

The parking lot itself is usually pretty well filled, but don't let this deter you. Most folks heading up from the trailhead are just gawkers who turn around after a few hundred yards. The next most popular destination is about a half mile away, and works well as a substitute tour if you or someone in your group runs out of steam or if the weather turns poor. The "Gravel Pit tour," as it is affectionately known, is a 1-mile round-trip hike that follows an old gravel quarry road up the White River Canyon, and ends at a man-made bowl.

If you're feeling more intrepid, head up a moderate hill from the south side of the gravel pit for an extra mile. The powerline you're passing under serves handily as the upper limit of a 3-mile round-trip hike. The lines provide the juice for the Mount Hood Meadows Ski Area, which is barely 2 miles to the northeast from this point. You can go just a little beyond the powerlines for a great view of Mount Hood.

Most skiers and snowshoers turn around here to make a 3-mile round trip. For a little variety, you can choose to cross the White River up here on the bluffs and descend back to the highway on the north side of the river. Again, if your legs will allow and you'd like to see more views of Mount Hood's alpine country, proceed even farther above the powerlines to reach a series of massive moraines. These imposing ridges were formed by the debris and sediment left from the White River Glacier, whose bottom end resides several hundred feet above timberline. It's even possible to climb

White River Trail

one of these moraines if the snow conditions are right. Be aware, however, that in sunny springtime weather the south-facing slopes of this canyon and the moraines above get heated up to a slushy consistency in the afternoons. That can lead to small wet avalanches that can endanger you even when the weather seems completely benign.

At about 4,800 feet the White River intersects with the Timberline Trail, a summer hiking route that leads to Timberline Lodge, just a few miles to the west. As tempted as you might be to proceed onward to the lodge, be aware that the route from White River Canyon to Timberline Lodge is riddled with avalanche hazard. It's not something to undertake casually or in anything other than bluebird weather. For starters, the Timberline Trail itself is largely obscured in the winter. Also, the route becomes confusing as you wind in and out of glaciers and moraines on your way to the popular ski area. You'd also find yourself marooned at the ski lodge without your car. While it's not a bad trip if you've arranged a shuttle and done the necessary preparation with map reading and are versed in alpine backcountry travel, it's much better to admire the alpine heights from the easy-to-locate canyon of the White River.

--10--
Trillium Lake Loop

Rating:	Moderate
Round trip:	5 miles
Starting elevation:	3,800 feet
High point:	3,800 feet
Best season:	December through March
Maps:	Green Trails No. 462, Mount Hood; USGS Mount Hood South; USFS Mount Hood National Forest
Who to contact:	Mount Hood National Forest, Zigzag Ranger District, (541) 662-3191

Trillium Lake is a classic winter sight, and not something you would expect to find so close to a highway. The wide sweep of the frozen lake surface lends a natural sense of drama that you might think exists only in nature calendars. In fact, Trillium Lake and the view of Mount Hood beyond has been featured prominently on hundreds of picture-postcards, book covers, and, yes, calendars. Once you get there you'll understand why. The broad expanse of the lake opens the skyline to reveal Oregon's tallest volcano in all its majesty.

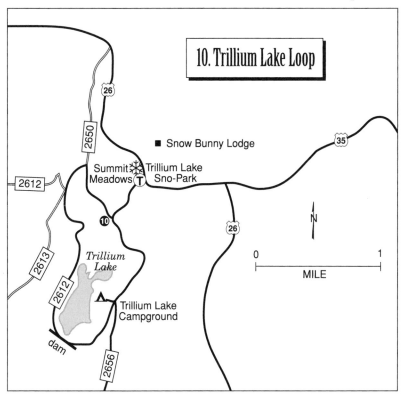

This route is unique in that it actually descends at the beginning. From the sno-park along Highway 26, the route drops more than 200 feet to the lakeshore, making it a great warm up for beginners. Also, because this route covers a snowed-over road, it's entirely accessible to all snowshoers, beginners and advanced alike. The total trip around the lake amounts to 5 miles, and aside from the initial drop into the lake basin, doesn't gain or lose much elevation. Nearly a half-dozen well-signed side trails and alternative loops dot this route. If you're trying to escape the possible crowds that can fill this lake basin on a typical winter weekend, consider following one of these side trails through the woods. Another caution: although it's practically overrun with snowshoers and cross-country skiers, this route is also open to snowmobilers, so keep an ear out for these fast-moving machines.

To get to the Trillium Lake Sno-Park from Portland, take Highway 26 southeast to Government Camp. Continue on Highway 26 past the eastern edge of town. The sno-park is located across the highway from the Snow Bunny Lodge. From the lot, snowshoe along the wide road down the hill

Trillium Lake

and watch out for the set tracks for cross-country skiers. There's enough room out here for everybody. The hill drops about 200 feet in half a mile, at which point you cross the junction for the loop. Most folks continue straight here in order to get to the lake's southern shore as soon as possible. It's at that point, just 2 miles from the trailhead, that photographers have been setting up their tripods for all those calendar and postcard shots. On your way there, pass on your right the entrance to the Trillium Lake Campground, which shouldn't be confused with other easier waterfront access points farther down the road. You will then pass Mud Creek Ridge Road (Forest Road 2656), a loop that covers 8 more miles and climbs out of the lake basin to views of the surrounding country, including Mount Hood.

Past the campground junction, climb a long but not steep hill to a viewpoint. The lake is just down the road from here. It goes without saying, but you shouldn't trust the frozen surface of the lake. The ice that may form there probably won't hold your weight and the risk just isn't worth the experiment. Stay on the shore and take some pictures or eat your lunch. It's the best view in the route. At 3,600 feet, cross the dam and continue the loop around the lake.

From the dam, climb a gentle hill (all hills on this route are gentle) and head for the Westside Divide, which is the junction for Forest Roads 2612 and 2613. Bear right and head for Summit Meadows, another scenic spot just 2 miles from the dam. Right past this junction is the site for pioneer graves, some of which date back well into the nineteenth century. Bear right again for half a mile to close the loop at the bottom of the route's first hill.

--11--
Yellowjacket Trail

Rating:	More difficult
Round trip:	6 miles
Starting elevation:	4,000 feet
High point:	4,800 feet
Best season:	December through March
Maps:	Green Trails No. 462, Mount Hood; USGS Mount Hood South; Mark Wigg, Mount Hood Ski Trails; USFS Mount Hood National Forest
Who to contact:	Mount Hood National Forest, Zigzag Ranger District, (541) 662-3191

It seems that almost as long as snowshoers have laid their webs to Oregon's snow, the Yellowjacket Trail has been considered a winter classic. Because of the terrain it crosses, this tour is considered demanding by cross-country skiers, but many of the skiers' concerns don't apply to snowshoers. Primarily, cross-country skiers worry about getting their spaghetti-noodle skis down steep hills, while snowshoers simply motor down them. The Yellowjacket Trail is indeed long and a little steep at times, but it's a great place for snowshoers to test their mettle and see some beautiful Mount Hood scenery along the way. The builders apparently suffered while mapping out this trail; it is named for the devilish insects that plagued the summertime trail-building project.

The route is traditionally done as a shuttle-drop trip, where hikers start from the junction of Timberline Road and Highway 26 after leaving another car at the White River West Sno-Park. If you choose to make a loop of it, you're in for a serious, demanding 16-mile adventure. The 6-mile trip from Timberline Road is taxing enough; making a full loop back there after getting to the White River area is something only very fit and prepared snowshoers should attempt.

There are many variations on the Yellowjacket Trail, and some guidebooks refer to the section between Highway 26 and the Snow Bunny cross-country ski trail as the "West Yellowjacket" Trail.

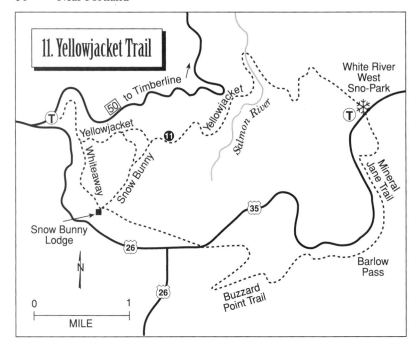

11. Yellowjacket Trail

White River
West
Sno-Park

to Timberline

50

Yellowjacket

Yellowjacket

Salmon River

Whiteaway

Snow Bunny

Mineral
Jane Trail

35

Snow Bunny
Lodge

26

N

26

Barlow
Pass

Buzzard
Point Trail

0   1

MILE

Those snowshoers who don't want to go all the way to White River can leave a car at the Snow Bunny Lodge. The tour would then end after about 4 miles but would bypass some great Mount Hood forest and hills. Again, this trail has its stout reputation for good reason; shoers attempting the mighty Yellowjacket should do so with solid preparations under their belt, including safety gear and fitness. Although the Yellowjacket area is well traveled, it's also potentially confusing because of the multiple trail options.

From Portland, take Highway 26 southeast about 90 miles to Government Camp. The trailhead is just a few hundred yards up the Timberline Road from Highway 26.

Hike east from the trailhead and cross Still Creek. From there you'll contour back out of that waterway's canyon and through beautiful older forest before just crossing the tip of Forest Road 226, also called the Whiteaway Trail. From there, hike another mile or so to the West Clearcut area and cross the upper end of the Snow Bunny Trail. If you want to head down to Snow Bunny, this is where you should turn right and south and head down about a mile and a half to the lodge. To continue on the Yellowjacket, go straight, even though you'll be paralleling the Snow Bunny Trail for a short while. Before long you'll dogleg back to the north and west and cross a broad flat expanse before crossing a fork of the Salmon River. From here you'll parallel the Salmon from atop a narrow ridge. The trail climbs to about 4,800 feet—a climb considered grueling for skiers trying to clamber up the hill on skinny skis—before dropping toward the river and crossing it. The Salmon is, at this point, only a river in name. Crossing the upper reaches of this stream is like hopping over a standard alpine stream.

Climb back out of the canyon and then descend through classic subalpine forest, but watch for the trail to turn to the north, eventually taking you to a meadow. Descend through open forest to about 4,500 feet then turn sharply to the east toward the White River Canyon. From here you can just drop into the canyon bottom and follow the river's course out to the parking lot. You'll know you're getting closer when you start to encounter other hikers and skiers and their multiple tracks. At this point it's worth a little prayer that not only have you stashed a car at the White River West Sno-Park, but also that you've stashed the keys to that car.

If not, or if you're feeling extra adventurous, then loop back to the Timberline Road area. Just be aware that it's another 10 miles away through sometimes unmarked trails. To do so, cross Highway 35 and follow the Mineral Jane Trail down toward Barlow Pass. From there, follow the Buzzard Point Trail and cross Highway 35 again before heading through unmarked forest to Snow Bunny Lodge. You can follow the Snow Bunny Trail back to the "West" Yellowjacket Trail and back to the Timberline Road parking area.

--*12*--
Barlow Pass

Rating:	More difficult
Round trip:	6 miles
Starting elevation:	3,900 feet
High point:	4,500 feet
Best season:	December through February
Maps:	USFS Mount Hood National Forest; Green Trails No. 462, Mount Hood; Mark Wigg, Mount Hood Ski Trails
Who to contact:	Mount Hood National Forest, Barlow Ranger District, (503) 467-2291

This route is a great cross-country hike that uses the Pacific Crest National Scenic Trail. In crossing from Twin Lakes over to the Barlow Pass area, you'll see a lot of the rugged wilderness for which Mount Hood's lowlands are famous. Climbing up from Wapinitia Pass gives you the sort of view that alternately confounds and delights Oregon wilderness enthusiasts: rolling evergreen forest, in this time of year frosted white.

Going from the Frog Lake Sno-Park to the Barlow Pass Sno-Park gives you a little more downhill terrain to cover on the way out. Use a shuttle for this route—rather than going back and forth—because there just isn't a simple way to make a loop out of it without killing yourself in the process. It's one thing to do an out-and-back trip from a base camp to a mountaintop; it's quite another to get to a sno-park and turn around again, and I don't recommend it on this tour. Just enjoy the straight northerly shot from Frog Lake to Barlow Pass.

To get there from Portland, take Highway 26 southeast to Government Camp. The Frog Lake Sno-Park is southeast of Government Camp on Highway 26. If you cross Blue Box Pass you've gone too far. The trailhead, which also leads toward Twin Lakes, begins at the north side of the parking lot and immediately enters the forest. That's a small saving grace because snowmobilers also use this sno-park. Fortunately, they're not allowed on the trail, and most of these motorized recreationalists head down the forest roads past Frog Lake and into the national forest. Snowshoers will head out on the Pacific Crest Trail, which is well marked, goes through the trees, and climbs gently.

Follow the marked trail uphill and to the east before switchbacking dramatically to the north after less than a mile of hiking. As you climb, notice the beautiful mountain hemlocks of substantial size. That's a significant achievement at these elevations; it's hard growing up there, no matter the season. The trail stays inside this sort of subalpine forest for much of the distance.

After a mile and a half the trail forks, and Trail 495 turns east toward the first of the two Twin Lakes. Continue north on the Pacific Crest Trail and begin climbing along the western flank of Bird Butte. Climb uphill, to the north, and you'll reach the hike's highest point at 4,600 feet. Northward! From here the slope empties out into a lightly forested plain before crossing a junction with the upper end of Trail 495. Again, push north here. After the trail junction, you'll be perched on a landform known in some circles as The Shoulder (4,500 feet), where you might actually peek through the treetops to view the summit of Mount Hood, to the north. Just off the trail to the east, you can view Devils Half Acre and Barlow Ridge, where Barlow Road passes.

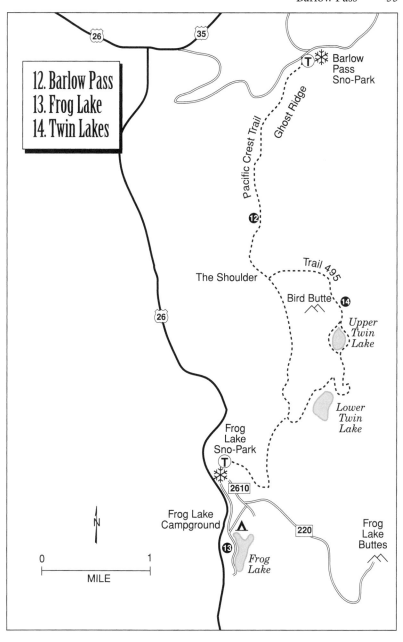

12. Barlow Pass
13. Frog Lake
14. Twin Lakes

Barlow Pass Sno-Park

Ghost Ridge

Pacific Crest Trail

12

The Shoulder

Trail 495

Bird Butte

14

Upper Twin Lake

Lower Twin Lake

Frog Lake Sno-Park

2610

Frog Lake Campground

220

Frog Lake Buttes

13

Frog Lake

N

0 1
MILE

Pacific Crest Trail sign at Barlow Pass

At this point you'll pass just east of Ghost Ridge, another great Mount Hood viewpoint. The top of Ghost Ridge is 4,800 feet and not a bad little extra grunt for the view. On top of Ghost Ridge on a good day you can see Mount Jefferson and down into the Trillium Lake Basin. It's also just about the only point on the tour where you will get above the trees and onto an open, windswept point.

From here and past the junction with Upper Twin Lake it's just over a mile down to the Barlow Pass Sno-Park. You'll know you've gotten off course if you go too far down either side of the shoulder.

--13--
Frog Lake

Rating:	Easy
Round trip:	1.5 miles
Starting elevation:	3,952 feet
High point:	4,000 feet
Best season:	December through March
Maps:	USGS Mount Wilson; Mark Wigg, Mount Hood Ski Trails; Green Trails No. 494, Mount Wilson; USFS Mount Hood National Forest
Who to contact:	Mount Hood National Forest, Bear Springs Work Center, (503) 467-2291

This route does a good job of clearing your head without requiring much of your legs, your preparation, or your ambition. It's perfect for snowshoers with small children who need to get out and who want to expose their kids to the outdoors without getting into a huge ordeal. Or you might just be traveling from Bend to Portland and need a brief opportunity to stretch your legs. Frog Lake is a popular sno-park for snowmobilers too, so don't bother with this area on a weekend. Come in the midweek, when you're more likely to have the peace you're after. Heavy snowmobile use does improve the route for snowshoeing in one way: they do tend to pack the road down quite well. That makes for easy travel with young ones. Still, walk to the side of the road in case motorized speedsters buzz past you.

From Portland, go southeast on Highway 26 to Government Camp. The route starts at the Frog Lake Sno-Park off Highway 26, just 4 miles south of the junction with Highway 35, which itself is east of Government Camp.

There are actually two ways to get to Frog Lake, so you can mix them up on the coming and going and create a loop. The most direct route is simply to get on Forest Road 2610 and follow it for less than a half mile, after which you turn right onto a side road, which ambles quickly and easily down toward the lakeshore. Even this road branches, however; the right junction curves around the western side of the lake, while the left junction is a more direct route to the lake. The first road to the left drops you out at the northern side of the lake, where you'll also shoe through the snowed-over Frog Lake Campground.

The other route to the lake starts on an unmarked primitive road, which directs you around the snowmobile highway of Forest Road 2610. This road cuts off just a few minutes out from the sno-park, turning right and climbing over a snow mound meant to block the route from snowmobile traffic. Follow this route for less than half a mile before it joins one of the aforementioned roads leading directly to the western shores of Frog Lake. You could make a loop of sorts out of this route by taking the older, un-marked road to the lake and returning via the campground access road and Forest Road 2610.

Feeling energetic? The climb up to Frog Lake Buttes offers great views after you've paid the price in elevation gain. The buttes stand at 5,294 feet and the 3-mile climb to their summit can be grueling for those not in shape. Skiers dread the return trip down from the buttes, but snowshoers shouldn't feel daunted in the slightest. To do this alternative trip, follow Forest Road 2610 to the turnoff at Forest Road 220 on the left, barely half a mile from the sno-park. Turn left and follow this road all the way to the top. You won't enjoy too many views on your way up, but once you are atop the Frog Lake Buttes, Mount Hood reveals itself in all its wintry glory.

--14--
Twin Lakes

Rating:	More difficult
Round trip:	8 miles
Starting elevation:	3,952 feet
High point:	4,400 feet
Best season:	December through March
Maps:	Green Trails No. 494, Mount Wilson; USGS Mount Wilson; Mark Wigg, Mount Hood Ski Trails
Who to contact:	Mount Hood National Forest, Bear Springs Work Center, (503) 467-2291

The Twins are a lovely pair of lakes in all seasons. They are nestled down in individual basins that are well insulated from foul mountain weather and highway noise. The two lakes also make a nice day trip for snowshoers looking for relief from the more crowded Mount Hood destinations. Whether it's because of the proximity of other, better-known routes such as Frog Lake or White River, or simply because there aren't a lot of jaw-dropping Mount Hood views, the Twin Lakes route rarely receives crowds of winter travelers. It's possible that skiers aren't interested in such an up-

and-down route or that they don't like skiing in the ungroomed, uneven snow surface in the forests around the lakes.

But if you've got the time, the Twin Lakes route is a great way to stumble across beautiful lakes barely 3 miles away from a parking lot.

From Portland, take Highway 26 southeast to Government Camp. The Frog Lake Sno-Park is southeast of Government Camp, just 4 miles south on Highway 26 from the junction with Highway 35. If you get to Blue Box Pass you've gone too far. The Frog Lake Sno-Park is well used by snowmobilers, but don't fret: motorized winter travel is prohibited on the trails that you'll access here. For a short distance you will, in fact, walk the Pacific Crest National Scenic Trail, which is easy to follow because of the trail markers nailed to trees at various points along the way.

Start at the northern end of the parking lot and immediately duck into a forest peppered with towering mountain hemlocks, a subalpine tree species that swells to impressive girth when it gets as old as these. You'll know them by their fine-needled sprays of branches and the many ripples in the dark bark.

Once on the trail, climb gradually through the forest for about a half mile before the trail takes a sharp turn to the north. Follow the trail as it contours northward around the hill. After a mile and a half, you'll meet a junction with Trail 495. The Lower Twin Lake is just a mile away, and if you're limited on time or energy, drop into the lake basin and take in the casual tour around the lake.

But if you so desire, you can keep going north on the Pacific Crest Trail for another 1.7 miles to the upper end of Trail 495. Take a right onto Trail 495 and walk east and eventually south for a mile and a half to Upper Twin Lake, at 4,400 feet. Pass through some beautiful old-growth forest on a descent, then climb again briefly to Bird Butte Pass at 4,500 feet. It's not long from here to the lake, which is just 100 feet lower in elevation. The small hump to the east of the lake, and Bird Butte to the northwest, dominate the view here, but Mount Hood is visible from the southern end of the lake. From Upper Twin you can walk south again toward Lower Twin Lake, which is barely short of a mile farther on Trail 495. But if you're looking for a more direct route, you can just point directly south toward the lower lake, descending a short steep hill to get there.

From Lower Twin Lake you can either continue on Trail 495 and return to the Pacific Crest Trail, or you can walk to the westernmost point of the lake and just muscle up hill, cross-country, back to the Pacific Crest Trail, which loops around the lake a few hundred feet above it.

--*15*--
Tom, Dick and Harry Mountain

Rating: More difficult
Round trip: Approximately 5 miles
Starting elevation: 3,400 feet
High point: 5,066 feet
Best season: December through April
Maps: Green Trails No. 461, Government Camp; USFS Mount Hood National Forest
Who to contact: Mount Hood National Forest, Zigzag Ranger District, (541) 622-3191

Cross-country skiers avoid this route because it is steep, has multiple switchbacks, and often gets rutted out. This makes it a great spot for snowshoers since these difficulties seldom hinder a determined 'shoer. The only skiers you're likely to see on top of Tom, Dick and Harry Mountain are backcountry telemark skiers who are after the bounty of powder that awaits in the bowls below the ridgeline summit. Never mind the ridiculous name, it's a spectacular location; the long ridge of Tom, Dick and Harry faces directly into the southwestern slopes of Mount Hood. (According to Lewis McArthur, author of *Oregon Geographic Names,* the mountain got its name because of the three distinct humps in its half-mile-long summit ridge.)

The trailhead is conveniently located at the Mirror Lake Sno-Park on Highway 26. You'll find it less than a mile from the western limits of Government Camp, which is approximately 90 miles southeast of Portland via Highway 26. The Mirror Lake Sno-Park is really just a wide spot on the sometimes-hectic Highway 26, so watch for the trailhead carefully. And because the trail is so close to town, that means within 5 minutes of finishing the route (which should take you about 3 or 4 hours to complete) you can be putting up your feet in one of that town's cozy watering holes.

Atop Tom, Dick and Harry's summit ridge, you may feel tempted to dash down toward Mirror Lake, but unless you've taken thorough measure of the day's avalanche hazard, don't risk it. The bowl is perfectly shaped, angled, and designed for a dramatic snow slide. That, of course, is precisely why backcountry skiers and snowboarders flock there. If you find safe conditions, which tend to prevail in the spring, challenge yourself to run down a steep slope like this without going head over teakettle on the way.

Tom, Dick and Harry Mountain

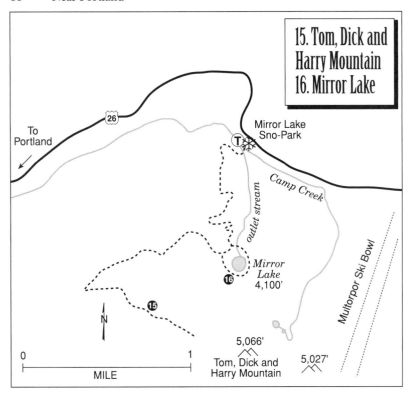

15. Tom, Dick and Harry Mountain
16. Mirror Lake

To Portland

26

Mirror Lake Sno-Park

T

Camp Creek

outlet stream

Mirror Lake 4,100'

16

15

Multorpor Ski Bowl

N

0   1
MILE

5,066'
Tom, Dick and Harry Mountain

5,027'

From the trailhead, go past Mirror Lake, which is a one-and-a-half-mile trip uphill on switchbacks through subalpine forests. The lake is lovely, but it's worth going past it to answer the call of Tom and Company's ridgeline views. To get to the summit, continue westward around Mirror Lake. The trail peters out along the base of a prominent northwest ridge, which is the most direct line to the top. The ridge will take you directly to the summit, but it also exposes you to wind and possible cornices as you ascend. Don't bother trying to ascend the prominent rock spire on the summit; instead skirt around its base and enjoy the views.

The top presents you with a view of Zigzag River Canyon to the north, below the glacier of the same name, and a view up toward Illumination Rock and Crater Rock, two landmarks on the most popular ascent route of Mount Hood. With a good pair of binoculars you might be able to monitor climbers and skiers on the mountain's upper slopes. To the south of Tom, Dick and Harry Mountain you can see down into the Wind Lakes basin and Wind Creek's canyon. From the summit of the ridge, you can also mount an ambitious side trip over to Multorpor Ski Bowl, an extra 2 to 3 miles away through the backcountry. This will work only if you've arranged a shuttle car or are willing to thumb a ride back to Mirror Lake Sno-Park. To get to Multorpor, stay at about the 5,000-foot level on the ridge that makes up Tom, Dick and Harry Mountain. If you follow this directly east, you'll wander into the ski area boundary, where you must use caution to avoid speeding downhill skiers. The upper portions of Multorpor are expert-level slopes, meaning that descending snowshoers need to watch out for drop-offs, icy steeps, and flying extreme skiers.

--16--
Mirror Lake

Rating:	Easy
Round trip:	3 miles
Starting elevation:	3,400 feet
High point:	4,100 feet
Best season:	December through March
Maps:	Green Trails No. 461, Government Camp; Mark Wigg, Mount Hood Ski Trails; USGS Government Camp
Who to contact:	Mount Hood National Forest, Zigzag Ranger District, (541) 622-3191

Here's a great little hike for several reasons. For starters, it's a good alternative for those of you traveling to Mount Hood with skier friends who will be bashing their knees at the ski areas; you can drop them off and pursue a little peace and quiet. Secondly, the route isn't so hard that you struggle all day, yet the view at Mirror Lake is a substantial reward. And finally, it's so close to Government Camp that you are within a few minutes of a hot chocolate as soon as you get back to the trailhead.

Watch the freezing levels before you head out for this trip, because it doesn't gain too much elevation. Fortunately, your proximity to Mount Hood gives you a lot of alternative routes if the snow is too wet at the Mirror Lake Sno-Park.

From Portland, take Highway 26 southeast to Government Camp. The sno-park is about a mile west of Government Camp's western entrance. It's really just a wide spot in Highway 26, so as you park or depart the sno-park, watch for speeding cars on the sometimes icy road. The trailhead is just across Camp Creek from the parking area. To get there, cross a short bridge that can be treacherous in icy conditions. Before you know it you'll be walking into the subalpine forests of Mount Hood, the sounds of traffic quickly fading as you climb the trail.

And climb you will. The trail climbs 700 feet in barely a mile and a half, just steep enough to cause cross-country skiers to think twice before climbing and descending this route. That works to your advantage because the crampons of most modern snowshoes will help you maneuver this trail—even in somewhat icy conditions. It should be noted that you can rent extra snowshoes at several ski shops in Government Camp. Call ahead on winter weekends to reserve a pair.

The trail crosses the lake's outlet stream almost immediately and heads south into the woods before switchbacking several times. Resist the temptation to cut the trail going up or down; doing so is hard on the terrain and disturbs the sanctity of the snowpack, which everyone has a right to enjoy in its unbroken state.

If conditions are right, you shouldn't discount some small possibility for avalanche hazard, even on this beginner's route. Especially as you approach the lake, remember some of the slopes you cross are open and the snowpack is resting only on open slopes. Again, because the route is relatively steep, you'll know you've gotten into the lake basin when the trail levels out at 4,000 feet. As you step out into the open lake basin, you will immediately be confronted with the beautiful crags of Tom, Dick and Harry Mountain. Watch for backcountry skiers who have climbed up to the upper reaches of that small peak to ski the bowls into the lake basin.

At the lakeshore, you have two options. One is to go to the left and again cross the outlet stream, to do the short loop around the lake, which is worth it. That's because on the western edge of the lake and up a little higher toward Tom, Dick and Harry's western ridge, you might be able to catch a view of Mount Hood, which is almost perfectly framed by the basin's steep walls. This, again, is another spot to watch for avalanches. Or call it good and take your lunch here, where afternoon sun lingers. Avoid walking across the lake; you can't tell if it will be frozen solid enough to support your weight.

Take your pick of several decent lunch spots (wherever the sun is shining). All sides of the lake have great open spots to plop down in the snow.

Mirror Lake outlet stream

--17--

Gumjuwac Saddle

Rating: More difficult
Round trip: 5 miles
Starting elevation: 3,600 feet
High point: 5,200 feet
Best season: January through March
Maps: Green Trails No. 462, Mount Hood; USGS Badger Lake; Mark Wigg, Mount Hood Ski Trails
Who to contact: Mount Hood National Forest, Hood River Ranger District, (541) 352-6002

This trail will test your mettle; it is a straight, unrelenting march up several switchbacks. Why bother? Because you will experience a beautiful, rugged part of the upper Hood River valley and stand on the edge of the Badger Creek Wilderness, a majestic and rarely visited part of the Mount Hood lowlands. In past visits to this terrain I've spotted hawks, owls, and bear tracks. There are a few opportunities for views across the Badger Creek area, and even Mount Hood might deign to show itself if the weather co-operates. For the more intrepid, a 3-mile round-trip extension will put you at the shores of Badger Lake. There's also the option of going the other direction for a 4.5-mile round trip up to Lookout Mountain at 6,400

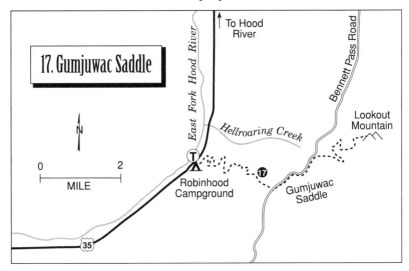

feet, which offers a great view of the mountain.

Take a map and compass for this route because it is not an "official" winter cross-country ski or snowshoe route, and therefore doesn't have any sort of blue markers on the trees. An altimeter is handy but not essential. Gumjuwac Saddle is really just a long north-south ridge between the Badger Creek and Hood River drainages. Bennett Pass Road, which travels the length of this ridge, serves as the abrupt western edge of the wilderness. It's a handy goal; get to the road and you've gone almost 2.5 miles before it's time to turn around and head back down the hill. And it's a steep climb, gaining 1,600 feet before hitting the saddle.

Near Gumjuwac Saddle

From Portland, drive east on U.S. Highway 30 to Hood River. Head south on Highway 35 for 28 miles to the Robinhood Campground. The trailhead is just a few hundred yards to the south and across the highway, on the eastern side of the road. Park right on the shores of the East Fork of the Hood River, a dynamic and bustling stream in any season. Walk across the slippery wooden trestle bridge and find the trailhead nestled against the northern end of another small parking area.

Enter a beautiful and misty forest of classic west-side Cascade species: western red cedar, Douglas fir, and ponderosa pine near the top of the saddle. The latter are evidence of the transition here between the wet west side of the mountains and the dryer east side. Standing at Gumjuwac Saddle will put you squarely on the dividing line between the two contrasting climates.

The trail has been dug deep into the side of this steep hill, so even in deep snow cover you should be able to follow its many switchbacks. Watch for hash marks in the trees and be aware of your position on the map and on the hill. At about 4,800 feet the switchbacks give way to a more direct easterly route; it's also at this elevation that you can rest on a bench of sorts for some small relief from the climbing. The route contours around the northern side of a shoulder here before switchbacking back up and to the east across the shoulder. At 5,200 feet pass just above the spring and headwaters of a small creek that feeds into Hellroaring Creek down to the north. Push on to the road and a junction for a variety of other trails that stretch out from here.

At this summit you've got several options. If your thighs are burning, turn and head back down to the trailhead. If you've still got something left in your legs, consider climbing north another 1,200 feet to Lookout Mountain; do so only if you're fit, if you're prepared for an extended trip in the mountains, and if daylight allows. The route to Lookout Mountain will take you at least an extra 2 to 3 hours, not to mention the hour it will take to get back down to the trailhead.

--*18*--
Opal Creek

Rating:	More difficult
Round trip:	7 miles
Starting elevation:	2,200 feet
High point:	2,400 feet
Best season:	December and January
Maps:	Green Trails No. 524, Battle Ax; USFS Willamette National Forest
Who to contact:	Willamette National Forest, Detroit Ranger District, (541) 854-3366

Experiencing this route on snowshoes is wonderful for two reasons: you will see a dramatic ancient forest under snow, and any winter when snow falls in these low elevations is a winter in which you will be doing a lot of good shoeing.

Opal Creek has been Ground Zero in Oregon's old-growth forest wars, in particular because it has inspired so many to rally to the cause of native forest conservation. A day spent in these woods will help you understand what all the fuss is about, and may inspire you to join in the fray. Some of

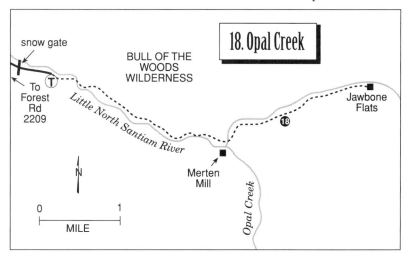

the trees in the drainage soar as high as 250 feet into the sky and are as old as 1,000 years.

If you're also just looking for a good scenic wander, this is the place. Although the route is simple—it takes place almost entirely on a road— the scenery is diverse and captivating. The massive trees in this drainage of the Little North Santiam River make up just a part of the diverse forest, with its varied shades of green. If you're lucky, a coating of white will dust the forest, although, I admit, this route rarely receives much snow. So watch the weather forecasts and the freezing levels in the Willamette Valley and if it gets cold enough and snowy enough, grab your snowshoes and head for Opal Creek.

To get to Opal Creek from Interstate 5 near Salem, drive east on Highway 22 toward Detroit. About 25 miles east of the Interstate 5 junction is the town of Mehama. Turn north onto Little North Fork Road, which leads you north to the Elkhorn Recreation Area. The road name refers to the Little North Fork Santiam River, which you will eventually hike alongside. Drive this road for about 21 miles; after about 15 miles the road shifts to federal management and becomes Forest Road 2207. At a junction stay left (which is almost straight) onto Forest Road 2209 and park at the locked gate.

Almost immediately upon leaving the parking lot you will notice that you are entering an ancient forest. On the north side of the road is the Bull of the Woods Wilderness, and to the south is unprotected national forest. The road continues past the locked gate; follow this route for 3 miles to the old mining camp of Jawbone Flats.

Just 2 miles upriver, at the intersection of the Little North Fork Santiam River and Opal Creek, pass the old site of Merten Mill, a defunct sawmill. From there you can scramble down to the water's edge for a view of the spectacular Sawmill Falls, a lovely sight in all seasons. But if you don't get sidetracked and you keep motoring up the road, you're just a mile and a half from Jawbone Flats, a funky and amiable old landmark. Most of the buildings here were built in the late 1920s and early 1930s, and they show their age. The mining has long since given way to forest education. For many years the owners and operators of the Shiny Rock Mining Company have been an integral part of efforts to preserve the forest of Opal Creek. Jawbone Flats has since become an educational site managed by the Friends of Opal Creek, but it still maintains its rough-edged charm.

The Three Sisters as seen from the Isaac Nickerson Loop

PART 2

Near Eugene

--*19*--
Gold Lake

Rating: Easy
Round trip: 4.5 miles
Starting elevation: 5,200 feet
High point: 5,200 feet at Gold Lake Sno-Park
Best season: December through April
Maps: Imus Geographics, Willamette Pass Cross-Country Ski Trails; USFS Willamette National Forest; USGS Waldo Lake
Who to contact: Willamette National Forest, Middle Fork Ranger District—Main Office, (541) 782-2283

A lot of beginner snowshoers and cross-country skiers share this route. It's popular among beginners for good reason: it's relatively short (you can do the round trip in about 4 hours), not too steep, and the scenery is rewarding for the short distance. On a clear day you can view the frozen lake itself and the hills around Willamette Pass, as well as Diamond Peak. A three-sided warming shelter at the lake is equipped with a wood stove and firewood.

To get there drive 67 miles east from Eugene on Highway 58. The Gold

Gold Lake outlet

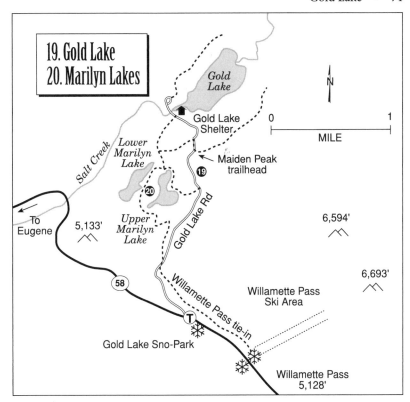

19. Gold Lake
20. Marilyn Lakes

Lake Sno-Park is located just below the summit of Willamette Pass on the right. At the sno-park you'll also find a warming hut constructed and maintained by the Willamette Backcountry Ski Patrol and U.S. Forest Service volunteers. When ski patrol members staff the hut, you can get good information about trail conditions. The Gold Lake Sno-Park also serves as a jump-off point for several other trips in the Diamond Peak Wilderness Area (and many routes in this book). On any given winter weekday you'll find several cars in the parking lot, and on weekends you'll be jockeying for a good parking space.

Once parked, walk (carefully!) across Highway 58 to Gold Lake Road. Watch for cars here; in winter the highway is often icy and treacherous. If you survive this first test, you're safe to don the snowshoes and head for the lake. The well-signed route follows a snowed-over road, which makes navigation virtually automatic in all but the worst weather conditions.

After a mile on Gold Lake Road, pass the Willamette Pass tie-in trail, a 1-mile connector to the Willamette Pass Ski Area parking area. You'll also

Gold Lake Shelter

pass the entry trailhead for the Marilyn Lakes Loop, which is a nice way to add a few miles to your trip if you like (see Route 20, Marilyn Lakes).

Because this route is so popular among cross-country skiers, it's especially important to observe the rules of trail etiquette and stay off their tracks. Besides, it's a road; there's plenty of room here for everyone.

Closer to the lake the route steepens slightly. This is more of an issue to cross-country skiers who may resort to using herringbone patterns up the hill. It's not a problem for snowshoers, who probably won't notice the grade's difference. At this point pass the Maiden Peak trailhead, which climbs steeply for 6 miles to the summit of that area landmark. Proceed downhill toward the lake. If you cross a bridge over a small, scenic creek, you've gone past the Gold Lake Shelter. It's hidden up on a small hill above the lake. A restroom, locked for the winter, is the first visible structure you see. Walk past it to the shelter to put up your feet.

Once at the lake, observe a key precaution: do *not* snowshoe on the lake, even if it looks frozen solid. There's no guarantee that any parts of the lake are solid enough to support a person's weight. Leave it to the ravens, which sometimes land on its surface to hop around in search of food.

The shelter is a great place to dry off, warm up, and eat lunch. Getting the stove started can be tricky but rewarding. Here's where the prepared hiker who always carries a lighter can show off his ingenuity. Just remember that the firewood needs to last all winter in case of emergencies. You'll thank other hikers if you're the one lost, tired, and wet. Finally, remember that the shelter is not intended for overnight stays.

--20--
Marilyn Lakes

Rating: More difficult
Round trip: 4 miles
Starting elevation: 4,800 feet
High point: 4,880 feet
Best season: December through March
Maps: Imus Geographics, Willamette Pass Cross-Country Ski Trails; USGS Waldo Lake
Who to contact: Willamette National Forest, Middle Fork Ranger District—Main Office, (541) 782-2283

The side trails to Marilyn Lakes offer a nice detour from the snow-traveler's highway of Gold Lake. If the popular Gold Lake Road is crowded, then duck into the woods and explore these lakes, which are beautiful gems tucked into the subalpine forests of Willamette Pass. There's a nice view of Diamond Peak from the northern side of Lower Marilyn Lake. And because the elevation gain is all but negligible, it's not that much of a difference to sneak off and explore these lakes. You can make a longer loop and drop down into Gold Lake from the Marilyn Lakes area and hike back via the road to Highway 58.

As do many other trails in the Willamette Pass region, this one starts from the Gold Lake Sno-Park on Highway 58. The sno-park is just a half mile below the actual summit of Willamette Pass, which is 67 miles southeast of Eugene and 70 miles southwest of Bend. The sno-park is also the home of the Willamette Backcountry Ski Patrol, whose members occasionally staff a small warming hut here. Here you can read the posted maps, use the bathroom, and, if someone is actually manning the station, get trail conditions or other advice.

Park here and walk carefully but expeditiously across Highway 58, listening for eighteen-wheel trucks that barrel down the pass like there's no tomorrow. Once you cross the highway, head about a half mile to the first junction with the Marilyn Lakes Trail. Four trails branch off Gold Lake Road heading up to the Marilyn Lakes area, but to make a full loop take this first cutoff. Descend the moderate, half-mile slope to the lake's plateau, at about 4,880 feet. March right between Upper and Lower Marilyn Lakes at this point. The trail leads you to the northern ends of the lakes and eventually loops east toward the northern toe of Upper Marilyn Lake. If you wander a little farther toward the tip of the lower lake you should be rewarded by a good view of Diamond Peak.

From here choose from a couple of options. At the junction with other trails you can walk to the right and back up to the Gold Lake Road, with another good viewpoint along the way. Or go left here and walk another half mile down to the Gold Lake Shelter on the shores of Gold Lake. There's even another trail down to Gold Lake Road along this trail; the options are endless, it seems. But to keep it simple, take either the first, shortest route back to the road; or for a longer trip, go straight down to the lakeshore and the shelter.

The shelter is like many in the region. It's a three-sided, beautiful log structure with a wood stove, a picnic table, and a hefty supply of wood that can be hard to light. From there it's a 2-mile walk back to the sno-park. Remember that even though the lake might look frozen solid, it's not a good idea to attempt to walk on it, even in snowshoes. There's just no guaranteeing at this low elevation that the ice will be frozen sufficiently to hold your weight.

--21--
Midnight Lake/Bechtel Shelter

Rating:	More difficult
Round trip:	Approximately 6 miles
Starting elevation:	5,000 feet at Gold Lake Sno-Park
High point:	5,400 feet at Midnight Lake
Best season:	December through April
Maps:	Imus Geographics, Willamette Pass Cross-Country Ski Trails; USFS Willamette National Forest
Who to contact:	Willamette National Forest, Middle Fork Ranger District—Main Office, (541) 782-2283

This route puts you just inside the Diamond Peak Wilderness via a short chunk of the Pacific Crest National Scenic Trail. The route to the lake is beautiful, but Midnight Lake itself is distinctly unspectacular, not much more than a clearing in the woods. There's the side benefit of having the Bechtel Shelter along a return route, should you choose to make a loop out of the trip. Whichever way you go, allow about 4 to 5 hours and enjoy the view of Diamond Peak, which dominates the landscape out here.

Use the popular Gold Lake Sno-Park and head in along the well-traveled Pengra Pass Trail. If you're here on a weekend, you can expect to see other snow travelers, but many people in this area seem to opt for the shorter routes of the Westview Loops. Although you might see some snow traffic headed to the Bechtel Shelter, it's not all that rare to have Midnight Lake to yourself.

To get to the Gold Lake Sno-Park, drive 67 miles southeast of Eugene or 70 miles southwest of Bend on Highway 58. The Gold Lake Sno-Park is just a half mile below the summit of Willamette Pass on Highway 58. From there, head toward Pengra Pass, noting the trailhead signs stating that skiers have the right of way on these trails (that just means stick to your own path).

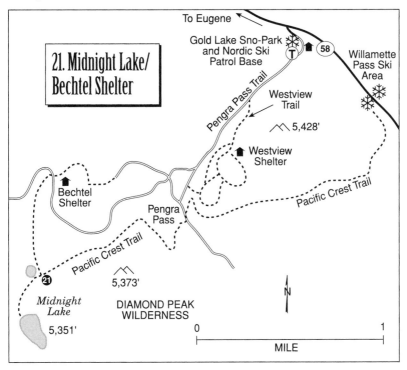

About a mile from the trailhead on the Pengra Pass Trail you will come to the junction with the Midnight Lake Loop. Along the way, at about the half-mile mark, pass the first Westview Loops trailhead on your left. This trail goes up into the forest toward the Westview Shelter, which is a nice short loop if you're already feeling tired. If Midnight Lake is still your goal, keep going straight here along the road to Pengra Pass. In a short distance, cross the first Midnight Lake Loop junction. Turn left and up the small hill. At the top, pass the southern trailhead for the Westview Loop. Carry on to the right and toward yet another junction, where a sign promises you that you'll get to Midnight Lake in 2 miles.

Here, finally, the road narrows into a trail, right before a sign to your right welcomes you to the Diamond Peak Wilderness. You are now on the Pacific Crest Trail; going left here would take you back toward Willamette Pass. Note here that within the wilderness area, blue diamonds no longer mark the trail. Instead, you will see quaint, hard-to-see wooden diamonds that nonetheless mark the trail very well if you keep your eyes peeled.

Climb up through a tight woodsy trail here and keep your ears open for descending, out-of-control cross-country skiers, especially in the spring when the trail is hard-packed and icy. As you climb the hill, get a view of the Willamette Pass Ski Area (across the highway) and of Bechtel Shelter, down in a clear cut across the small valley. In a mile or so, step out onto a wide bench in the topography, where you cross the junction for the Bechtel Creek Trail near a tiny frozen lake. Keep that junction in mind for the way back. The lake itself is now less than half a mile away.

On the way out, take a left turn at the Bechtel Creek junction and cross out of the wilderness (you can tell you're out of the wilderness when the blue diamonds start reappearing on the trees). This new trail will drop you back out on what's known as Abernathy Road, and you could take it straight back to the sno-park. But it's worth the digression to go to Bechtel Shelter. Turn right on Abernathy Road regardless, but watch for the Bechtel Creek Trail, a poorly marked side trail to the left and down to a clearing where the shelter sits.

From the shelter, you could take the thin trail across Bechtel Creek and back toward the main road you came in on. Or you could go back up to Abernathy Road and head east for the sno-park, which is a little more than a mile away.

Midnight Lake Loop, with Diamond Peak in the distance

--22--
Salt Creek Falls

Rating: Easy
Round trip: 5 miles
Starting elevation: 4,000 feet
High point: 4,400 feet
Best season: December through February
Maps: Imus Geographics, Willamette Pass Cross-Country Ski Trails; USGS Waldo Lake
Who to contact: Willamette National Forest, Middle Fork Ranger District—Main Office, (541) 782-2283

Even if you don't have time for a full-blown snowshoe expedition, you must at least stop, get out of your car, and look at Salt Creek Falls. The stunning, 280-foot falls mesmerize you with their constant plunge to the creek bottom. If it's cold enough, you'll see the dramatic and bizarre ice formations created by the constant duress of water slamming down upon them. The name of the creek stems, apparently, from the area's natural mineral springs and salt licks that were used by deer. From the parking lot, take a viewpoint trail that leads along the canyon for several impressive perspectives on the landmark cascade. Watch for ice, pack your camera, and enjoy the spectacle.

For more of an outing, take Salt Creek Road, a relaxing tour through intermittent pastures and meadows. Little elevation gain makes this an easy tour, even though the full round-trip distance is 5 miles.

To get there, head east from Eugene on Highway 58; Salt Creek Falls Sno-Park is the first you'll encounter. The sno-park is about 60 miles from

Salt Creek footbridge

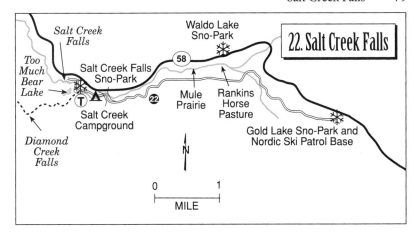

Eugene and about 20 miles east of Oakridge. The parking lot sits at 4,000 feet, making this one of those west-side Cascade routes that requires a low freezing level and consistent cool temperatures to be feasible for snowshoeing. If temperatures even approach freezing at this elevation, take advantage of that window of opportunity and try out this nice, even route, perfect for novice snowshoers as well as families with younger children. If all else fails, you can at least make the 200-foot trek to the waterfall viewpoints.

Salt Creek Road is a relatively straightforward hike along a gently undulating road until it ends about 2.5 miles up the way. If you're considering a more ambitious tour, stay on Salt Creek Road for about 4 miles or so. (You must set up a shuttle for this route.) You will eventually reach the Gold Lake Sno-Park.

Start the Salt Creek tour by hiking along a trail through the Salt Creek Campground. Before you cross Salt Creek, turn right and east, paralleling the sno-park's access road before you connect with Salt Creek Road. You cross Salt Creek on a large bridge soon after getting onto the road. At this point you have an option to take a quarter-mile side trip. Going left on a cross-country ski trail and crossing Salt Creek immediately would put you on a trail in the woods to Too Much Bear Lake, a landmark whose name begs for a good storytelling. Odds are the person who named that lake spent a sleepless night there, but the story is buried in Oregon's history books. The lake is a lovely spot surrounded by (frozen) rhododendron bushes and is a great short jaunt of only about one quarter mile, if road tours aren't to your liking and you'd rather be in deeper woods. In a mile and a half up this trail, the hard-to-see landmark of Diamond Creek Falls is a nice goal; there are well-built viewpoints all along the trail, and if the fog lifts enough you can see the falls as they wash over a gradual drop-off.

After the trail connects with Salt Creek Road, follow it about 2.5 miles until it turns into a more primitive road that leads to Gold Lake Sno-Park. That's an ambitious tour without a shuttle, but something to consider if you're feeling up to it. Otherwise, a tour on Salt Creek Road might go just 2 miles up to the flatlands and meadows. At the Rankins Horse Pasture, a couple miles up Salt Creek Road and just down the hill from the Waldo Lake Sno-Park across the highway, the elevation is a mere 4,500 feet, which gives you another reason to monitor the forecast and the freezing levels before you set out.

--23--
Maiden Peak

Rating: Most difficult
Round trip: 16 miles
Starting elevation: 4,800 feet
High point: 7,818 feet
Best season: December through March
Maps: Imus Geographics, Willamette Pass Cross-Country Ski Trails; USGS Waldo Lake; USGS The Twins; USGS Odell Butte
Who to contact: Willamette National Forest, Middle Fork Ranger District—Main Office, (541) 782-2283

When asked to recommend a solid, challenging route near Willamette Pass, I'll always answer "Maiden Peak!" This is a tough route, one that should not be undertaken lightly. It's one of those trips that you can brag about when finished and point to frequently when you're on other hikes in the Willamette Pass region. But you'll need more than ego inflation to fuel your trip to Maiden Peak. I'd say go because you'll get unparalleled views of the central Oregon Cascades and other prominent landmarks. Or do it because you want to see just how far your legs can go in a single day. I've limited the possible season for this route to March, though in reality most Oregon snow years allow you to chase the summit of Maiden Peak well into June. If you're lucky, you can drive the Gold Lake Road and start hiking from there, or if you have a season's pass to Willamette Pass Ski Area, operators may let you ride their chair lifts to the base of this prominent butte. Otherwise, you're in for a stout haul that demands an "alpine start," (i.e., early in the morning) and plenty of snacks and water.

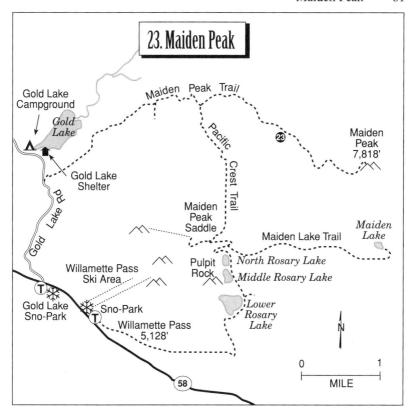

Most Maiden Peak expeditions start from either the Gold Lake Sno-Park or the Willamette Pass Sno-Park. The former parking area is about 67 miles from Eugene going southeast on Highway 58. The latter is less than 2 miles farther up the pass (on the left-hand side if you're driving east). The Willamette Pass Sno-Park also serves the bustling Willamette Pass Ski Area, so avoid the place on weekends if you can help it. The parking lot fills to capacity on snowy weekends.

There are two ways to do the trip. The more direct route takes you from Willamette Pass up the Pacific Crest National Scenic Trail and past Rosary Lakes to the Maiden Lake Trail. It's 7 miles just to this landmark, still about a mile from the top at this point. The simplest thing to do, once you've hit Maiden Lake, is to just point your snowshoes uphill and start marching. By the time you hit Maiden Lake, you're on the flanks of Maiden Peak, and because it's really just a volcanic cone, you can't wander off the mountain and get lost. Just push uphill through ever-shorter forests of mountain hemlock and whitebark pine until you hit the summit of Maiden Peak.

The top of this mountain is an old lookout site, and if you're lucky enough to climb it in decent weather, you can see why. It's a beautiful landmark.

The other way to do the route is a little more grueling, although it's almost exactly the same distance. This way is harder because it lacks the "scenery breaks" that Rosary and Maiden Lakes offer. It's nonetheless a fine route to the top and is marked for winter travelers the whole way. To get to Maiden Peak from this alternate route, first hike the 2 miles to Gold Lake, then turn off at the well-marked Maiden Peak Trail, located barely half a mile south of the Gold Lake Campground. Pass the Skyline and Pacific Crest Trails, but disregard either junction if you're headed to the top of Maiden Peak. Attack the western flank of the mountain from this angle and be aware that on a sunny, late-spring day the snow can get maddeningly wet in the late afternoons. Try this route after a fresh snowstorm has passed, when the snow is lighter and easier to displace. There are few switchbacks; instead the trail pushes unrelentingly to the top—straight up through the dense forests—and pops you out on the cinder cone's summit with views all the way to southern Oregon on a good day. Mount Hood, Mount Thielsen, and perhaps even the Three Sisters will greet you from the summit of this trail. Remember, the top of Maiden Peak is just the halfway point. If you're thinking of doing a loop of the trip, start from the Rosary Lakes and Maiden Lake area and return via the Gold Lake Trail. Going the opposite way would require you to be more precise in your routefinding, just to get to the Maiden Lake Trail.

--24--
Fuji Creek Trail and Shelter

Rating:	More difficult
Round trip:	8 miles
Starting elevation:	4,400 feet
High point:	5,600 feet
Best season:	December through March
Maps:	Imus Geographics, Willamette Pass Cross-Country Ski Trails; USGS Waldo Lake
Who to contact:	Willamette National Forest, Middle Fork Ranger District—Main Office, (541) 782-2283

It's almost criminal, the bounty of views that can be had on a route this straightforward. From the Fuji Creek Road and the shelter at its summit,

Fuji Creek Shelter

Diamond Peak is resplendent in all its alpine glory. This is one of those routes that makes forest lovers feel guilty for loving a clear cut. The logging done here in the last decade has left behind dramatic openings in an otherwise impenetrable forest, which in turn leaves incredible views where snowshoers might otherwise only see a wall of trees. The Fuji Creek Road is also an anomaly in that it is one of few roads that poke into the Waldo Lake Wilderness neighborhood; although you're not in the wilderness proper on this tour, you are in some pretty fine country.

This route can be done as a loop with a shuttle assist, or as an out-and-back. Either way, start from the Salt Creek Falls Sno-Park, where you can safely park your car and start the tour. Although you must cross the highway, it's easier than trying to park your car on snowy Fuji Creek Road.

Salt Creek Falls is just 58 miles southeast of Eugene on Highway 58. Park your car here, head back up the sno-park entry road toward the highway, and cross over to the Fuji Creek Road. You can also pick up a trail that parallels the sno-park road, as if you were headed up the Salt Creek Falls route (Route 22). But instead of turning right when you meet up with Salt Creek Road, turn left and cross the highway.

At this point, the tour is a fairly straightforward hike up a snowy road, which steadily gains elevation over a relatively short distance. After a few switchbacks, the road turns to the east at about the 1-mile point. Get your camera out here, because the next 1.7 miles to the shelter turnoff boast

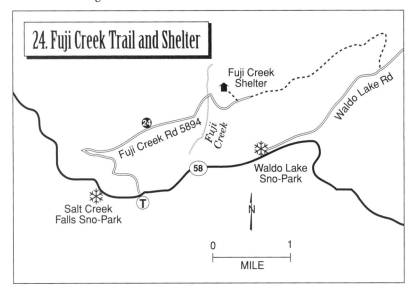

24. Fuji Creek Trail and Shelter

some splendid views that are worth blowing film over. The terrain here is the usual western Oregon patchwork of young regrowing trees and older forest. The views of Diamond Peak, Willamette Pass, and Maiden Peak are all stellar along this upper portion of the road.

After you cross Fuji Creek the road starts to level out, and before too long you should start looking for the trail to the Fuji Creek Shelter, which is off to the north or left of the road. Follow the blue diamonds to the shelter, which is one of few in the area actually built for sleeping. Although it's a three-sided affair, there is also a sleeping loft above the wood stove, which is a great place to throw down a warm sleeping bag and spend the night. The missing wall is perfectly located to take advantage of Fuji Mountain's great views of the surrounding peaks. It's easy to while away an afternoon here, and potentially an entire evening if you've got the proper overnight gear. Don't count on having enough firewood; if you plan to spend the night you should take a camping stove for cooking and melting snow for drinking water. Also, don't expect a quiet night in the wilderness; from the cabin you can hear trains huffing up the steep tracks over Willamette Pass on the south side of the highway. It's either romantic or annoying, depending on your perspective.

From here the trail continues on Forest Road 5894 before it turns into a trail that contours along the same level for a few miles, before dropping to the Waldo Lake Road in about 2 miles from the cabin. When you finally reach the Waldo Lake Road, it's still another 2 miles to the Waldo Lake Sno-Park where your shuttle should be waiting.

--25--
Rosary Lakes

Rating: More difficult
Round trip: 8 miles
Starting elevation: 5,200 feet
High point: 5,700 feet
Best season: December through March
Maps: Imus Geographics, Willamette Pass Cross-Country Ski Trails; USGS Waldo Lake
Who to contact: Willamette National Forest, Middle Fork Ranger District—Main Office, (541) 782-2283

Religious overtones aside, this is a great hike that passes through some beautiful older forests on the saddle of Willamette Pass. You can tell you're getting closer to Oregon's east side here, because the forest is dotted with larger ponderosa pine, a sign of the drier climate on east side of the Cascades. Some trees in the forest here are truly massive; others have moss draped over their boughs like loose-fitting robes. In the winter, especially after a fresh snowfall, snow piles up on the wide branches of the older trees. You can do this route in less-than-perfect weather; because you'll be insulated from wind and weather in the woods on the way up to the lake. What's more, you don't get the full effect of the crag known as "Pulpit Rock" until it's shrouded in mist. If you're the churchgoing type and you do this route on a Sunday, seeing the rock might make you feel a little bit guilty if you're snowshoeing when you should be in church. I leave the moral dilemmas up to you. Meanwhile, this is a great route for intermediate snowshoers who can handle a few hundred feet of elevation gain and a sideways-sloping hill that requires some nimble stepping on steeper parts.

You can choose to start the route from the Willamette Pass Sno-Park, approximately 70 miles southeast of Eugene on Highway 58. The other parking option is a quarter mile east on Highway 58, behind the Oregon Department of Transportation storage sheds. Park at Willamette Pass Ski Area unless it's really crowded; doing so allows you access to the ski lodge for hot drinks, a bathroom, or a telephone, if needed.

From the Willamette Pass Sno-Park parking lot, hike past the Sleepy Hollow chair lift, the easternmost base chair at the resort reserved for beginners and kids. A trail picks up in the woods just behind the lift, and a sign declares that it's 4 miles to Rosary Lakes. It's about a mile from here to

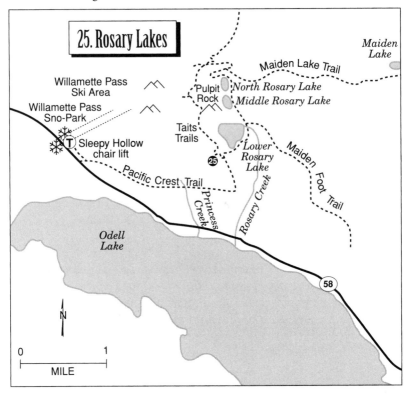

25. Rosary Lakes

Maiden Lake

Willamette Pass Ski Area

Maiden Lake Trail

Pulpit Rock

North Rosary Lake

Middle Rosary Lake

Willamette Pass Sno-Park

Taits Trails

T Sleepy Hollow chair lift

Lower Rosary Lake

25

Maiden Foot Trail

Pacific Crest Trail

Princess Creek

Rosary Creek

Odell Lake

58

N

0   1

MILE

the Oregon Department of Transportation sheds and the Willamette Pass Trailhead. From here the trail quickly connects with the Pacific Crest National Scenic Trail and begins climbing steadily uphill and to the east.

Within a couple of miles you should start to see the huge ponderosa pine that mark the transition zone to the east side of the Cascades. They're distinguishable from the other evergreen fir trees by their long needles in bunches of five and orange-yellow bark. These trees take up a lot of space in the forest canopy, with wide outstretched branches.

By about the second mile up the hill, the trail takes a sharp turn to the north, at 5,600 feet. You're now within shooting distance of the Lower Rosary Lake, and the trail begins climbing steeply here. In another 180 feet of elevation gain, come across a junction with the Taits Trails, below a sizeable rocky ridge. If you go left here you would climb more steeply uphill and over behind Pulpit Rock, closer to the ski area's boundaries. Instead, go right and come across the shores of Lower Rosary Lake, where there's a stunning view of Pulpit Rock.

Like all lakes in the Willamette Pass area, the Rosary Lakes may look frozen solid, but don't walk on them. You can't ever be certain that they're solid enough to hold your weight.

From here continue north on the trail to the Middle and North Rosary Lakes. Around the northern side of the lower lake cross a trail junction with the Maiden Foot Trail, which drops back down toward Odell Lake. Go straight for a little over a mile, then cross the other lakes and hit the Maiden Lake Trail. It seems like few people ever go to Maiden Lake, and you might even be breaking trail to Rosary. But if you like, go another couple of miles to Maiden Lake from here. To do this, stay the course to the Maiden Peak Saddle. That gets you up to about 6,200 feet and from there you can loop back around behind Pulpit Rock and bear left to get back to the Rosary Lakes–Taits Trails junction.

Rosary Lake and Pulpit Rock

--26--
Waldo Lake

Rating: Most difficult
Round trip: 18 miles
Starting elevation: 4,400 feet at Waldo Lake Sno-Park; 5,000 feet at Gold Lake Sno-Park
High point: 5,400 feet
Best season: December through March
Maps: Imus Geographics, Willamette Pass Cross-Country Ski Trails; USGS Waldo Lake
Who to contact: Willamette National Forest, Middle Fork Ranger District—Main Office, (541) 782-2283

This wintertime classic gets you in for a look at the second-largest fresh-water lake in the state of Oregon. Waldo Lake is a local landmark known for its pure waters. In recent years, however, motorized boat activity has tarnished that second designation. Still, in the winter, Waldo Lake's size makes it a stunning sight. This route to Waldo Lake could have earned an "easy" rating if it wasn't for the distance.

Waldo Lake was apparently named for Judge John B. Waldo, who was known as an aficionado of the surrounding area, especially the mountains. In fact, the Waldo Glacier on the southeast slope of Mount Jefferson was also named for him, according to Lewis McArthur, author of *Oregon Geographic Names*. In the nineteenth and twentieth centuries the lake went through a few name changes. It was first called Virgin Lake, then Pengra Lake before taking on its current moniker.

Unless you can cover this substantial distance in 1 day (which is tough, given the reduced amount of light in the winter) prepare to camp out by the lakeshore to do this trip in a safe and sane manner. That way you'll enjoy what the trail and the lake have to offer. There is a shelter at the lake, which is not necessarily intended for sleepovers.

There are two ways to do this trip, and both have advantages and draw-backs. The first and most direct route is to park at the Waldo Lake Sno-Park, about 67 miles southeast of Eugene on Highway 58. Start marching up snowed-over Waldo Lake Road for 7 miles to the Waldo Lake Trailhead. The only problem is the trek along this road can get a wee bit tedious. It's also a popular snowmobile route, which can make for some busy traffic on winter weekends.

The quieter but more complex route is a 2-day journey with an overnight at South Waldo Shelter. Start at the Gold Lake Sno-Park, just 3.5 miles farther down Highway 58 from the Waldo Lake Sno-Park. Head for Gold Lake, and then proceed past on a tie-in trail toward Waldo Lake Road. From the shelter at Gold Lake, it's less than a mile to the Waldo Lake Road. On this route you can avoid snowmobiles for a substantial amount of the road, and also you can use the Gold Lake Shelter as a break point along the way. From the shelter, cross the bridge over the Gold Lake outlet stream and pass through the campground. Go straight at a junction in the trail; there is a proposed ski/snowshoe route that parallels the Waldo Lake Road, but at this time it's not been built and is a little hard to follow. Climb

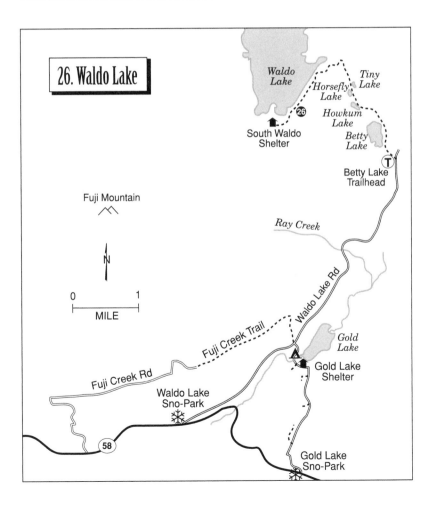

Waldo Lake Road

out onto Waldo Lake Road just down from the Fuji Creek Trail up to that area's shelter. Motor on up the road for another 1.8 miles to the trail to Betty Lake and beyond, to Waldo Lake.

From the Betty Lake Trailhead it's 2.5 miles to the shores of Waldo Lake. You'll first pass Betty, which is a nice-sized lake in it own right, then Howkum Lake, a tiny and oddly named lake off to the left of the trail. There's also little Horsefly Lake and, last but not least, Tiny Lake bordering the trail before you reach Waldo Lake.

The South Waldo Shelter is on the southern end of the lake, a few hundred yards off from the actual lakeshore. The shelter is well hidden from view and is surrounded by tall trees. From this shore you should be able to see Mount Ray in the distance to the south. You should also know that you're on the eastern boundary of the Waldo Lake Wilderness Area. The slopes to the west climb up toward Fuji Mountain.

--27--
Fawn Lake

Rating:	More difficult
Round trip:	7 miles
Starting elevation:	4,800 feet
High point:	5,600 feet
Best season:	December through March
Maps:	Imus Geographics, Willamette Pass Cross-Country Ski Trails; USGS Willamette Pass; USGS Odell Lake
Who to contact:	Deschutes National Forest, Crescent Ranger District, (541) 433-3200

It's a namby-pamby sort of name, but the scenery from this lake is nothing short of stunning, and this seldom-traveled route is a great alternative to the Crescent Lake area. Amazing craggy peaks surround you as you stand near or on Fawn Lake. The snowboarders or skiers in the group will drool over the beautiful slopes on Lakeview Mountain or Redtop Mountain. Both are wonderful, overlooked smaller peaks in this countryside dominated by Diamond Peak. Try this trail if you're looking for an alternative to the busier trails of

Fawn Lake Trail

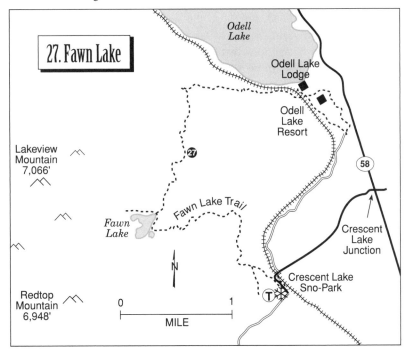

the Willamette Pass area and have good weather for taking pictures.

Because it's not so heavily used, however, this trail isn't always broken before you, and the markings on the trees aren't always clearly visible. Because this area was included in the Diamond Peak Wilderness, many of the blue diamond markers that used to be on the trees have been removed and replaced by simple wooden markers. That makes it even more important to carry a map and compass on this route, because you'll have to do a bit of routefinding. Also, if it hasn't snowed in a while, the thick forest that covers much of the route can make for an icy snow surface in the woods. Be ready for some slippery sidehill hiking on this route.

Start by driving to the Crescent Lake Sno-Park, which is on the east side of Willamette Pass, approximately 70 miles southeast of Eugene. From Highway 58 turn right at the Crescent Lake Junction. The road here isn't very good and is rendered a little more hazardous by the presence of snowmobilers who mob the Crescent Lake area. Not to worry, they'll disappear as soon as you get onto the trail. The sno-park is just 2 miles off Highway 58. The map there isn't all that helpful, so be sure to bring your own.

From the northern end of the sno-park, head west on Fawn Lake Trail, which parallels the road for less than half a mile before crossing a snowmobile road and re-entering the forest. There is an old cut, similar to a powerline trail, which can potentially confuse you if you're the first up the trail. Bear right and walk up the side of the slope to the north. Enter a mixed forest that starts out in ponderosa pines and assorted fir trees. Before long, however, lodgepole pines dominate the dense forest. At the 5,200-foot mark turn to the west; the trail begins to level out in the lodgepole forest. Walk through gently undulating forest here before you reach the lakeshore at just over 5,600 feet.

The summer hiking trail winds around the eastern shore of this lake, and if you can find an easy way down to the shore, take it. Get the best views of the surrounding crags from this eastern side of the lake. From there, the most dramatic-looking peak to the west is Lakeview Mountain, which tops out at 7,066 feet. To the south of that landmark is Redtop Mountain, a beautiful but more rounded-out peak than Lakeview Mountain. Redtop's summit is at 6,948 feet and both of the peaks hide

Snowshoe frisbee on Fawn Lake. Do not try this at home.

some secret backcountry skiing and snowboarding stashes. It's still a good mile and a half away just to the base of them, so if you're thinking of extending the trip to include a summit of Redtop, make sure you budget in the extra time and effort required.

You can choose an alternate, 11.4-mile loop by carrying on north on the summer trail and following the wooden markers as they take you 4.5 miles toward the Odell Lake cross-country ski trails. You are forced to cross the railroad tracks here before turning east and hiking the remaining 3.5 miles back toward the Crescent Lake Road. Take care crossing the railroad tracks; it's shockingly easy to catch a snowshoe in them. What's more, trains are moving plenty fast by the time they get to this spot, and the snowy woods insulate the noise of an oncoming train, (which you might not realize until the train is just about on top of you). From the Odell Lake Resort trails, the route parallels the train tracks all the way back to the sno-park.

--*28*--
Diamond Peak

Rating: Most difficult/backcountry
Round trip: 8 miles from Corrigan Lake Trailhead
Starting elevation: 5,000 feet
High point: 8,744 feet
Best season: February to June
Maps: USGS Diamond Peak; USFS Willamette National Forest
Who to contact: Willamette National Forest, Middle Fork Ranger District—Main Office, (541) 782-2283

This classic spring ascent is a rare gem. It's "doable" by relative newcomers to backcountry snowshoeing, yet challenges experienced mountaineers. It's unlikely that you'll wear the snowshoes the whole way up; in fact, crampons and ice axes are recommended. If you wait until the road to the Corrigan Lake Trailhead is open a good ways, you'll save miles and time and get to the real climbing that much faster. In "typical" Oregon snow years, this may not occur until May. When the road is open that far, you can get up and down in a single day because it's only about 4 miles from the trailhead to the top.

In fact, the Corrigan Lake route is one of several ways to the top of

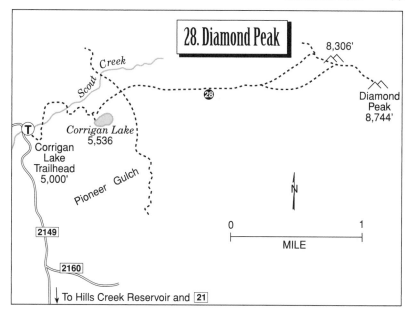

28. Diamond Peak

8,306'

Creek

Scout

28

Diamond
Peak
8,744'

Corrigan Lake
5,536

Corrigan
Lake
Trailhead
5,000'

Pioneer Gulch

N

2149

0   1
MILE

2160

To Hills Creek Reservoir and 21

Diamond Peak. In midwinter, an ambitious tour starts at the Gold Lake Sno-Park and passes westward by Midnight Lake, across alpine ridges that go past 7,100-foot Mount Yoran, and on to Diamond Peak for a total of 10 miles one way. That's a strenuous 3- to 4-day trip. For the rest of us, the Corrigan Lake route offers quick springtime access to the west side of Diamond Peak. On the way up you'll also pass through magnificent old-growth forests of Douglas and subalpine fir.

That same beautiful forest, however, makes navigation in the winter or even late spring a bit of a challenge. You must carry a map and compass, and perhaps even an altimeter. The other challenge you'll face on this route is the dramatic avalanche hazard on the mountain's west face. Although it's not unheard of to climb right up this steep face, doing so without making a thorough analysis of avalanche hazard is asking for trouble. Also be aware that in some years, alpinists leave orange flagging along the more direct routes to the top. These routes might be more direct, but they won't always follow the old summer trail's path. This can create problems if you ignore your map and compass in your desire to follow the flag line. If the flagging should disappear, it can take you a while to find out where it's dropped you off. So always watch the map, even if the route seems obvious.

To get to Corrigan Lake, first drive from Eugene southwest to Oakridge on Highway 58. Then drive south from Oakridge on Forest Road 21 past the Hills Creek Reservoir. Follow this winding road for about 30 miles to Forest Road 2149. This is where you'll find out just how far you'll be walk3 miles you'll pass the junction with Forest Road 2160. The Pioneer Gulch route, which follows the summer hiking trails 3630 and 3690 just up Forest Road 2160 from this junction, is yet another way up, but it's not quite as scenic. Don't turn right here; instead, keep going on Forest Road 2149 toward the Corrigan Lake Trailhead, which you'll meet in another 2 miles.

From here the trail winds up through tall trees. In the late spring, there's likely to be a lot of downed timber along the trail. Since there are a few switchbacks on the trail in the summer, watch the terrain and use your compass. It's just about 2 miles to Corrigan Lake, where you'll get a good view of Diamond Peak. Sadly, the lake, a lovely spot, is only at 5,536 feet, which means you still must climb roughly 3,000 more feet.

From Corrigan Lake aim just about due east, toward the massive bowl that fronts Diamond Peak's west side. Before you break out from the trees at the base of this bowl, you'll need to make a decision about avalanche hazard, your group's abilities, and your determination to get up to the summit. This is your last chance to either take the safer and smarter route, which is up the long southwest-facing ridge that starts above Corrigan Lake, or just go straight up the gut of the mountain. The southwestern ridge is a good line to the summit, but take care to stay on the north side of the ridge and follow it up past timberline. Crampons are necessary here: on this route you're forced to traverse some steep slopes that can be icy on early spring mornings. Cross a fat saddle before making the final push to the summit. From this saddle you can also peer down into the bowl that is so favored by backcountry skiers and snowboarders. In fact, if it's a sunny weekend day in the spring, you can just about count on seeing a few *glisse* artists ply this face.

As many of the Cascades do, Diamond Peak can get awfully icy toward the summit. From the top, you can see Oregon's mountains in all directions. Find a windless spot on the top where you can enjoy an early lunch and contemplate the thousands of feet of elevation you've just gained. Heading down, you can once again choose your own adventure; picking your way back down the southwest ridge makes perfect sense. For the intrepid (and well prepared), the bowl offers unsurpassed glissading from the lower saddle. Just make sure you can stop yourself before you get going too fast.

--29--
Potato Hill

Rating: Easy
Round trip: 3.5 to 4 miles
Starting elevation: 4,100 feet
High point: 5,207 feet on Potato Hill summit
Best season: January through March
Maps: Imus Geographics, Santiam Winter Recreation; USFS Willamette National Forest
Who to contact: Willamette National Forest, McKenzie Ranger District, (541) 822-3381

The Hash Brown Loop, which you will follow for this trip, is a great Sunday walk, something you could attempt after an early brunch that featured this loop's namesake food item. On a good day, Potato Hill offers excellent views of central Oregon's "smaller" volcanoes, such as Three Fingered Jack and Mount Washington. On a cloudy day you might choose to be as

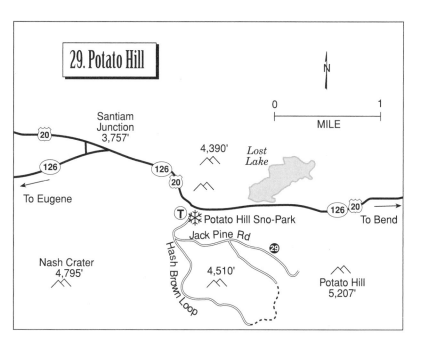

View of Three Fingered Jack from the summit of Potato Hill

foolish as the author and wait around on Potato Hill's summit for a good hour just to get a glimpse of Three Fingered Jack's craggy summit ridge.

Otherwise, in cloudy or sunny weather, the Potato Hill area offers classic older forests of Douglas fir, and a bit of easy hill-climbing on Forest Road 830, which is also known as Jack Pine Road. For those with limited time, energy, or skill, a simple march up and down the road, which is easy going, could suffice as a 3- to 4-hour introduction to snowshoeing. Potato Hill was the site of a dramatic fire earlier in this century, the Airstrip Burn, which left a large patch of the hill looking pretty barren. This does several things. First, it opens up the area for great views. Second, it tempts the energetic snowshoer who might want to run downhill through the open sections. Third, it threatens that same snowshoer's knees with buried stumps. Have fun, but play it safe.

To get to the trailhead, drive 80 miles east from Eugene on Highway 126; take the turns for Highway 20 and continue toward the Santiam Pass summit. The Potato Hill Sno-Park is located a mile from that junction. It's not much of a sno-park, really, just a wide spot in a sometimes busy—and in the winter, usually treacherous—road. Above the plowed area you will find plenty of room to lace up the snowshoes.

From the sno-park walk up Jack Pine Road for less than half a mile. Reach your first junction, which should be well signed and may very well have a map. Depending on the weather and your interests, you can either go straight up the road and head for the summit of Potato Hill, or turn right and first cover the forested section of the trail. Most days I head right, or eastward, and uphill because I'm eager for the good views up above. The summit of Potato Hill is another mile and a half up Jack Pine Road. Along the way, watch for a good view of Mount Washington to the south. Pass a second junction for the Hash Brown Loop a half mile from the first one. Go straight ahead toward the top. You'll have to come back down to the junction to complete the loop.

The road may peter out before you reach the summit of Potato Hill. A large expanse of young replanted conifers just below the true summit should allow fine views if you've no interest in the bona fide summit. From there, head back to that second junction, which will drop you down through the old burn and into the older forests of the Santiam Pass area. This portion of the loop meanders for another 2.3 miles through the woods before reconnecting with Jack Pine Road. The entire trail is well marked with blue diamonds on the trees, but if you're the first one here after a heavy snow you can count on doing some woodsy routefinding.

--30--
Maxwell Butte

Rating:	More difficult
Round trip:	8 miles
Starting elevation:	3,690 feet
High point:	4,300 feet
Best season:	December through March
Maps:	Imus Geographics, Santiam Pass Winter Recreation; USGS Santiam Junction
Who to contact:	Willamette National Forest, Detroit Ranger District, (541) 854-3366

For an area that's as extensively marked, groomed, and maintained, the Maxwell Butte trails don't get nearly the attention of other trail centers in this region. The trails here are almost dizzying, there are so many junctions and twists and turns. This description should be a good start to exploring the area, which has loop and trip lengths for all types of snowshoers.

One unexpected benefit of the extensive clear cutting that went on in this area is that it has allowed for some decent views of the surrounding

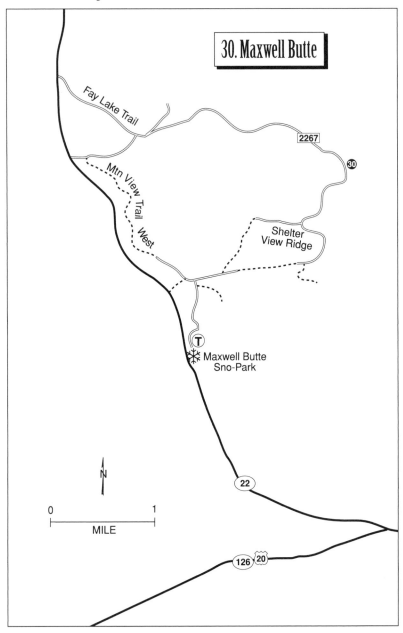

30. Maxwell Butte

Fay Lake Trail

2267

30

Mtn View Trail West

Shelter
View Ridge

T

Maxwell Butte
Sno-Park

N

0   1
MILE

22

126 20

mountains. Where you do encounter older forest, the trails take on an
entirely different character. The loop is well named, at least in clear
weather. From the high point you can get excellent views of Three Fin-

Maxwell Butte trails

gered Jack, Mount Washington, the Three Sisters range, and if you're tall enough, you can just barely make out a view of the top of Mount Jefferson.

The Maxwell Butte Sno-Park is located on Highway 22 east of Salem, about 3 miles west of the junction of Highways 20 and 22. The large parking area is fully equipped with bathrooms and area signs, but carry your own map so you're not relying on the often-confusing route markers on the trail itself.

For starters, take the northwestern-most trail access point, conveniently located behind the bathrooms. Enter a beautiful older forest that, sadly, doesn't last for long. Follow the trail north, shadowing the highway for less than a mile to the first junction. At the junction step onto the Mountain View Trail, known here as the "Mountain View Trail West." Walk alongside a recently clear-cut area, which consequently offers great views of the mountains. In 1.5 miles connect with the junction for the northern side of the Mountain View Loop. If you're getting tired, turn around here because after this point you'll be committing to the loop.

Turn east here and march along the loop's northern edge for about 4.3 miles. In about a half mile you'll pass a junction for the Fay Lake Trail, but you should carry onward. Follow the course of Forest Road 2267, which climbs to about 4,000 feet for much of its distance. Be aware that there are multiple turnoffs and "tie" trails that lead west toward Shelter View Ridge. If you stay the main course, Forest Road 2267, you'll pass just below the summit of Shelter View Ridge, the top of which is at 4,320 feet. From here, it's a panorama of Oregon volcanoes. If the weather is clear, shoot a few souvenir photos from this ridge.

Now take on the south leg of the loop through a clear cut, down through intact forest, and back down toward the first trail junction. Again, cutoffs abound here, and if you like you can take a tie-in trail over to the Maxwell Sno-Park Loop and head back to the parking lot this way. But to keep it as simple as possible in this maze, head back to the first junction with the western leg of the Moutain View Loop. From here, things should look familiar; turn back south and head through the older forest back toward the sno-park.

--31--
Prairie View Loop

Rating:	More difficult
Round trip:	5.5 miles
Starting elevation:	3,200 feet
High point:	3,350 feet
Best season:	December through March
Maps:	Imus Geographics, Santiam Winter Recreation; USFS Willamette National Forest
Who to contact:	Willamette National Forest, McKenzie Ranger District, (541) 822-3381

This is a good trail to take some snowshoe "newbies," or beginners, on because of the negligible elevation gain, moderate terrain, and impressive views of the surrounding Oregon peaks. Also, even though the views of the mountains are at times stunning, you're never far from the highway if things go wrong for some reason. The Prairie View Loop is one of those routes that makes good use of some haphazard land management. The route weaves in and out of clear cuts and regrowing logged areas and also uses logging roads for some of the trails.

The Isaac Nickerson, or Ikenick, Sno-Park is northeast of Eugene on Highway 126, barely 3 miles southwest of the junction with Highway 20. It's a small parking area, so be careful when you're pulling into the small space.

From the sno-park head up the main road and take your first right turn in a few hundred yards. For the next 1.3 miles the trail undulates gently as it passes through mixed forest. Meet the next junction in a meadow, where you should be able to see Ikenick Creek. Turn left, cross the creek, and head forward and up a mellow grade on what is now a snowmobile track.

Then come to the next junction, which is a quick cutoff that shortens the loop dramatically, if you need it. Taking a left would mean traveling 0.2 miles across to Road 673 or Forest Road 2672. Both numbers are visible on the signs.

To complete the full loop, ignore this cutoff and proceed straight toward a junction with the northern tip of the loop trail. If you go straight, you'll be headed toward Fish Lake in just a few hundred more yards. Follow the loop to the left and away from the highway noise. I presume that the territory you're on at this point is what is known as the "prairie," but it's really just a very low-growing forest with occasional clearings. Cross two creeks before coming to the Prairie View Extension Trail and the option to go right to get to Highway 20. Instead of going right, go left here to return to the sno-park in the shortest period of time. Or you can choose a nonmotorized route that will reconnect with the snowmobile road in another 1.6 miles. Here again you pass in and out of beautiful mixed forest and then through clear cuts that are attempting to regrow. At the second junction of the nonmotorized route, you've got less than half a mile to go before you turn back toward the sno-park. Here you will see a partially buried sign (in heavy snow years) that reads "Highway 126" with a pointer. The Three Sisters, Mount Washington, and Three Fingered Jack all spring into view at this point, perhaps when you're most tired.

Prairie View Loop

From this junction, push on about a mile back toward the sno-park along a well-traveled snowmobile road. Be aware that because the snow-

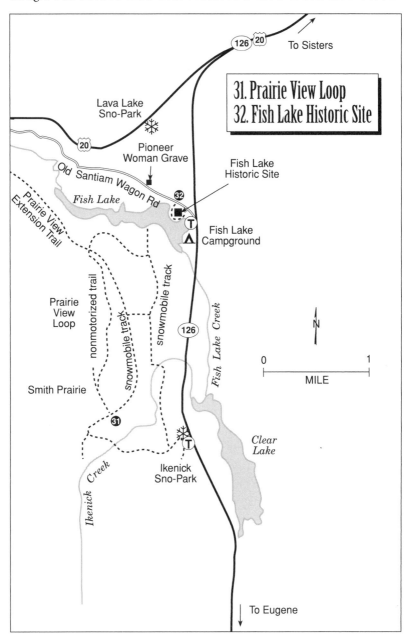

mobile track twists and turns, snowmobile travelers might not see you when you're tramping down the road. Exercise caution and try to stay on the side of the road if you hear them coming.

--*32*--
Fish Lake Historic Site

Rating:	Easy
Round trip:	1 mile
Starting elevation:	3,100 feet
High point:	3,200 feet
Best season:	January to March
Maps:	Imus Geographics, Santiam Pass Winter Recreation; USFS Willamette National Forest
Who to contact:	Willamette National Forest, McKenzie Ranger District, (541) 822-3381

This is definitely one of those Sunday afternoon rambles with the kids, with an opportunity to catch up on some Oregon pioneer history along the way. Winter's really the only time to see Fish Lake anyway, since in the

Fish Lake

Fish Lake Historic Site

summer the darned thing often dries up completely. But in late winter it's a lovely 1-mile-long lake that you can certainly loop around. If you're going to make this a stop on a trip between Bend and Eugene be sure to get a look at the old cabins and structures that date back well into the nineteenth century.

There aren't yet any trails here per se, so your options vary. Some of the structures and sites here are relics from the state's earliest days. For the U.S. Forest Service, this site represents some of the agency's first Oregon outposts.

This area isn't developed as an official sno-park, so watch carefully for the two possible parking areas along Highway 126. Coming east from Eugene, the Fish Lake Campground is almost exactly 1 mile before the junction with Highway 20. It's directly across the highway from a distinctive lava flow. Note, however, that the parking lot isn't maintained for winter use and may be little more than a turnout on the side of the road. Be careful pulling off the highway, which can be icy in midwinter. If this turnout is occupied or too dicey for your car, the other option is to park at the Ikenick Sno-Park and start your hike on the Prairie View Loop. Follow this trail about 1.5 miles north until you come to the primitive road that accesses the Fish Lake Historic Site.

From the campground turnout, walk north to the Fish Lake Historic Site, which includes a collection of ancient buildings. In the latter portion of the nineteenth century, the Fish Lake area was a stopover on the Santiam Wagon Road, portions of which are still marked. Some of the old wooden buildings date back to 1892, according to research done on historic photographs. The U.S. Forest Service, newly established at that time, built the

Fish Lake Guard Station as a base of operations for pack and saddle stock travels. The old place took on new prominence in 1910, when it was used as the summer headquarters for the old Santiam National Forest. If it's a good winter and snow levels are high, you'll be able to walk above the windows of the buildings and maybe even peek inside. They're well maintained even though they're in the process of falling apart.

The old Santiam Wagon Road, which was built in the 1860s long before the guard station, goes right through here. Follow it past the log cabins and come to the gravesite of Charity Ann Marks, a pioneering Oregonian who died here, tragically, just after giving birth to a child in 1875. The Santiam Wagon Road continues from here up to Highway 20 through a beautiful forest of massive older trees, where it connects with the Prairie View Extension Trail. That trail heads back along the west side of Fish Lake before connecting to the Prairie View Loop in 1.7 miles. You could do this as a loop, and follow the southern shores of Fish Lake back to the parking area, if you so desire. Remember though, that once you leave the Prairie View Extension Trail you'll be off a marked trail and must follow the lake's edge to get back to the campground. Watch also for deceptive lake edges; it's easy to find yourself thigh-deep in water that you may have thought was solid snow.

Here the U.S. Forest Service rents out well-maintained cabins, where you can spend a cozy night by Fish Lake. Contact the McKenzie Ranger District for reservations. Call early because these cabins quickly fill up with skiers and snowshoers.

Hayrick Butte

Rating:	Backcountry
Round trip:	4 miles
Starting elevation:	4,800 feet
High point:	5,000 feet
Best season:	January through March
Maps:	Imus Geographics, Santiam Winter Recreation; Geo-Graphics, Mount Washington Wilderness Map
Who to contact:	Deschutes National Forest, Sisters Ranger District, (541) 549-7700

You might feel a bit sneaky on this route because you'll start in the hustle and bustle of the Hoodoo Ski Area, but before long you'll be escaping into

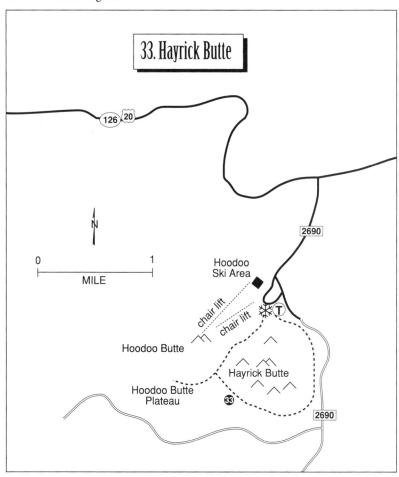

the backcountry and far from the madding crowd. The circular path of this route offers much in the way of solitude and views, and also gives the native Oregonian a new perspective on a familiar area.

This route gets a "backcountry" rating only because it doesn't follow a well-marked road or even a trail for much of the hike. But with that said, navigating this route is relatively simple, and the rule of thumb is clear: if you get too far from the hulk of Hayrick Butte, you're off route. That's all there is to it.

Hayrick is an impressive hunk of topography, with its steep sides and virtually flat top. There's no route to the top that doesn't expose climbers to serious avalanche hazard, so don't bother trying. What's more, beware

Hayrick Butte

of getting too close to the base of Hayrick, because avalanche hazard here can be considerable. Remember that even if you get away from the absolute base of the butte, you could still expose yourself to hazard. An avalanche doesn't need much of a running start to travel a long way out from the bottom of the hill, so pick your route around Hayrick carefully.

To get there, drive on Highway 126 east from Eugene or west from Bend to the Santiam Pass summit. Turn in at the sign for Hoodoo Ski Area. Start the route in the parking lot of Hoodoo Ski Area. You should attempt to park on the far southeast corner of the ski area's parking lot, near the maintenance sheds. There's a chair lift, but you'll be walking along the eastern border of the ski area. Hayrick Butte immediately announces its presence, towering over this part of the ski area. You may have to scurry past some flying skiers here, but if any of them get to where you are down at the base of Hayrick, they're going to need your snowshoes to get back to the ski area. The ski area's boundary is right along the base of Hayrick, and there is a skier's trail that skirts along the base of the ski area. Walk the base of Hayrick and begin shadowing its lower flanks.

You basically want to point your snowshoes toward the gap between the two buttes of Hoodoo and Hayrick. There are great views from here of Mount Washington. This is something of a low-elevation pass, with open slopes below you. If you continue south and angle a bit to the west, you'll come out onto the Hoodoo Butte Plateau, a beautiful area. You can follow an old roadbed right to this spot. The road eventually leads to the summit of Hoodoo Butte, a place to avoid when the ski season is in full swing.

This area is the site of an old burn, and that's why much of it has such an open, treeless feel. In the distance to the south, snowmobile routes follow the track of the old Santiam Wagon Road across the meadows. You won't go that far; instead drop down into the meadows, but stay within a safe distance of Hayrick and angle east by southeast. I doubt you'll get above 5,000 feet on this route.

If you were to go directly east, you would find yourself on Forest Road 2690, which is a snowmobile route back to the Ray Benson Sno-Park. Instead stay close to Hayrick and avoid the noise and hazard of the snow machines. If you stay on the same contour levels throughout this route, you can get back to your car without much of a navigational challenge.

--34--
Old McKenzie Pass (Highway 242)

Rating: More difficult
Round trip: 12.5 miles
Starting elevation: 4,000 feet
High point: 5,324 feet
Best season: January through April
Maps: USFS Deschutes National Forest; Geo-Graphics, Three Sisters Wilderness Map
Who to contact: Deschutes National Forest, Sisters Ranger District, (541) 549-7700

This route leads you to the summit of the McKenzie Pass, where the views of the Three Sisters are superb. The mountains are so close you might think you could climb them without much extra effort. However, if you feel like you have it in you, a trip of the entire distance (almost 40 miles) from Sisters to McKenzie Bridge on this road is an Oregon classic. For now, let's concentrate on the McKenzie Pass, which is a long but satisfying route. It's 6 miles each way, however, so schedule an early start time. In fact, when you stand wearily atop the McKenzie Pass, you have gone only one-fifth of the entire route across the old highway.

The Old McKenzie Highway is closed to vehicle traffic in the winter by formidable snow gates, leaving it entirely to you and your snowshoes. By following a road, you should be eliminating much of the navigational chal-

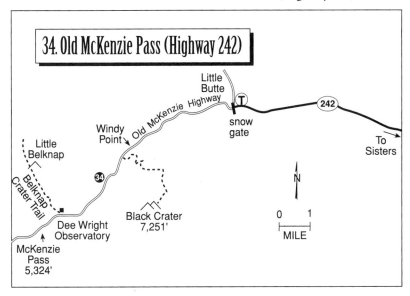

34. Old McKenzie Pass (Highway 242)

lenge. But be aware that during a snowstorm this place becomes devilishly hard to navigate because of the thin subalpine forests that often give way to large lava fields. When visibility is poor it can be fairly easy to wander off the road and into the Three Sisters Wilderness. Consider taking this trip in the spring when the road is closed, the days are longer, and the weather is milder. What's more, the harder spring snow speeds up snow-shoe travel considerably.

To get there, travel west from the town of Sisters on Highway 242 as far as you can go. The snow gate is located 8.5 miles from town, at 4,000 feet. But in a heavy snow year the snow can stop your car's travel sooner than the snow gate. Watch your odometer to see how many extra miles you'll have to travel to get to the snow gate. Park as best you can off the main road, and begin walking here.

It's a long first couple of miles on the road, because you'll be in the forest and the scenery doesn't quite show itself yet. Keep the faith: at the 3-mile mark (about 4,900 feet) reach Windy Point and get a glimpse of the mountains. On a good day you can see both Jefferson and Washington to the northwest. Remember that you've got about 3 miles, and an elevation gain of about 400 feet, before you reach the pass.

Windy Point also marks the beginning of your passage next to a massive lava flow, which has the effect of opening up the landscape for more views of the surrounding country. There's plenty to see here, including a view to the southeast of Black Crater, which rises to 7,251 feet. From here the road winds and dips through the lava flow, and it's in this territory that you need to watch where the road is going. Again, if the weather turns foul you should seriously consider turning back, especially if you aren't totally comfortable with navigating by map and compass alone.

Just before you reach the absolute summit of the pass, come alongside the Dee Wright Observatory, which in the summer is a tourist attraction. In the winter it just looks like a funny little stone building. At the observatory cross into Lane County from Deschutes County (you might be able to see that sign as well).

When you reach the observatory, you're pretty much at the pass, and the upper limit of this portion of the Old McKenzie Highway. The lava fields flow in all directions here, and the mountains take up massive portions of the horizon (North and Middle Sisters are the most prominent). A trail to Belknap Crater also takes off from here, and you might feel inspired to wander the lava fields.

-- 35 --
Isaac Nickerson Loop

Rating:	Easy
Round trip:	4 miles
Starting elevation:	3,200 feet
High point:	3,500 feet
Best season:	January and February
Maps:	Imus Geographics, Santiam Winter Recreation; USFS Willamette National Forest
Who to contact:	Willamette National Forest, McKenzie Ranger District, (541) 822-3381

The Ikenick Sno-Park, whose name is a marginally clever short form of the name Isaac Nickerson, accesses some great, well-marked beginner loops. There's even the prospect of a skier–snowshoers' shelter getting built on this particular loop. Until then, the best part of this trail, which you can do in about 2 hours, is a view of the Three Sisters mountains, which is worth putting on the cover of a scenic calendar. Rarely do you get such a perfectly framed view of those three beautiful mountains. That also gives you a hint of why the forest service and local touring groups plan to put a shelter here.

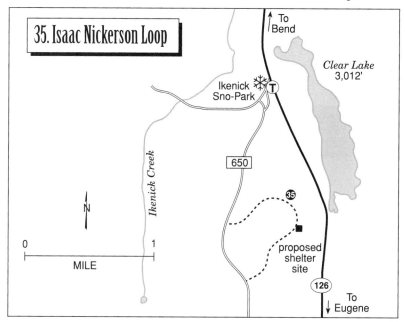

35. Isaac Nickerson Loop

To Bend

Clear Lake
3,012'

Ikenick Sno-Park

Ikenick Creek

650

35

N

0   1

MILE

proposed shelter site

126

To Eugene

The Ikenick Sno-Park is located on Highway 126 less than 3 miles before its junction with Highways 22 and 20. It's one of the most well-signed sno-parks around, with big maps and a lot of blue diamonds to spare. In the summer the "trails" here are really just old logging roads, but in the winter that just makes most of the loops easy to follow.

Start the Isaac Nickerson Loop either by sneaking off into the woods to the south of the parking lot or by simply following the main Road 650 past the snow gate. If you go through the woods, just follow blue diamonds for about 10 to 15 minutes before you hit the road again. If you take the road out of the sno-park, bear left at the first junction.

After a mile on Road 650, come across a clear cut full of younger trees. Watch for the marker here; the trail goes left into this young grove, toward a wall of older, darker forest. But once inside the younger and shorter forest, look to the north for a great view of Three Fingered Jack, which looms over this area. To the right of Three Fingered Jack, glimpse Hoodoo Butte, a small ski hill near the summit of Santiam Pass. Continue through the clear cut toward the top of a small hill before re-entering the older forest on a road. Trek a short distance through this pretty older forest, then come to another regrowing clear cut. North Sister fills your field of view here. In fact, if you crane your neck just right, you'll get a partially obscured view of

Isaac Nickerson Loop

Three Fingered Jack, Mount Washington, and the Three Sisters all in a row.

Continue on a short uphill through the woods before the clear cut drops away steeply to reveal a glorious view of the Three Sisters range. This is the halfway point of the loop and possible site for the future shelter. From here, the trail winds around toward the south, skirting the boundary between the older forests and the young regrowth of recent clear cuts. A half mile from the shelter site, come to Road 650 again. Turn right here and head back toward the snow gate and your car. As you march back toward the trailhead along this road, a great view of Three Fingered Jack will keep your mind off any sore feet or wet clothing.

PART 3

Near Bend

--*36*--
Tumalo Mountain

Rating: More difficult/backcountry
Round trip: Approximately 4 miles
Starting elevation: 6,375 feet
High point: 7,775 feet
Best season: December through May
Maps: Geo-Graphics, Three Sisters Wilderness Map
Who to contact: Deschutes National Forest Headquarters,
(541) 383-5300

Tumalo Mountain gets a "backcountry" rating simply because it has no visible trail in winter. Otherwise this is a great, straightforward little climb up to one of the best views in the Three Sisters country. You can do the trip in about 4 to 5 hours. Its location is advantageous for a number of reasons.

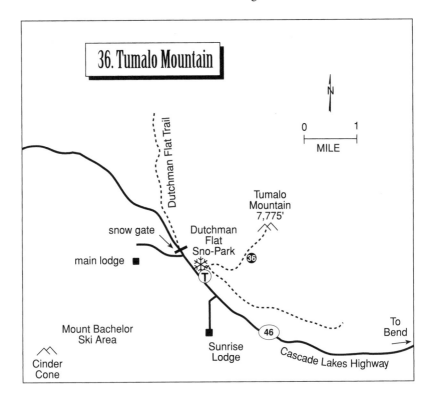

Because it's the only conical butte besides Mount Bachelor across the road, it's hard to get lost on its flanks. What's more, it's right across the road from the Mount Bachelor Ski Area, giving nonskiers in the group a chance to coordinate a day of snowshoeing with their friends' desire to go skiing. Most of the scenic photographs you see in Mount Bachelor catalogs were taken from the top of this little mountain. In less than 2 hours of climbing this gradually sloping butte, you'll face dramatic views of the Three Sisters mountains as well as a panoramic view of Oregon's high plateau.

Tumalo Mountain

To get there from downtown Bend take Highway 46, also known as the Cascade Lakes Highway, almost 21 miles southwest to the Dutchman Flat Sno-Park. You'll be just up the road from the west entrance to Mount Bachelor Ski Area. Snowmobilers and cross-country skiers also use this parking lot, so be prepared for traffic. Fortunately, snowmobiles are prohibited on the southern slopes of Tumalo Mountain (that's where you're headed), and only the hardiest telemark skiers will be climbing to the top. The north-facing bowl at the top of Tumalo Mountain offers outstanding backcountry skiing opportunities.

But you're here to snowshoe. To do so, walk across the lot to the edge of Tumalo's flanks and begin climbing. There is a trailhead marker at the western edge of the parking lot, but it's mostly for the users of the Dutchman Flat meadows and cross-country ski trails beyond. From that sign, head north by northeast up the hill.

In the summertime, the trail to the summit of Tumalo Mountain is approximately 1.5 miles. In wintertime the trail is buried, so you can take as direct a route as you like. Your best bet is to follow your nose and your compass to the top of the butte. You're likely to cross other paths on the

On the way to Tumalo Mountain

way. Just above the parking lot is a snowmobile track that you'll have to cross to get up into the quieter woods. During your first hour in the forest, mark your progress toward timberline by gauging the height of the trees. The sparser and shorter the trees become, the closer you are to the summit. Proceed north by northeast through the forest and emerge into an open meadow below the final few hundred feet to the top.

Although your final destination, the summit, is now visible, your next obstacle is a couple hundred feet of hiking through dense frozen trees, which are usually completely coated in rime ice. Routefinding through these trees can be difficult; I usually find success by contouring around the hillside to the east. Once atop the summit, be careful not to walk too near the edge of the bowl. In most heavy snow years, the summit of Tumalo Mountain holds a dramatic cornice over the northeast ridge that could release under a snowshoer's weight. On a windless day, which is rare up on Tumalo, the summit makes a grand location for a lunch with a view. You can look across the highway at the skiers fighting for space on the slopes of Mount Bachelor and be glad you chose a quieter activity. You also may see telemark skiers or backcountry snowboarders making their turns in Tumalo's bowl, which is a magnet for those who are willing to hike for fresh powder. If the wind is howling, consider taking your lunch break in the meadow back below the summit knob. For your descent, return the way you came, although you can parallel your route in another section of the forest. Just be wary of uphill ski tracks, and try not to disturb those.

--37--
Swampy Lakes Trails

Rating:	Easy to moderate
Round trip:	Variable
Starting elevation:	5,800 feet at Swampy Sno-Park
High point:	6,000 feet
Best season:	December through May
Maps:	USFS Deschutes National Forest; USFS Swampy Sno-Park Nordic Ski Trails
Who to contact:	Deschutes National Forest, Bend/Fort Rock Ranger District, (541) 383-4000

Ask Bend locals where to go snowshoeing on a winter's day, and they're likely to tell you to head for Swampy Lakes for two reasons. First, the Swampy Lakes Sno-Park accesses many trails of widely varying difficulty. And second, it's a good place to tell tourists to go so locals can have their secret

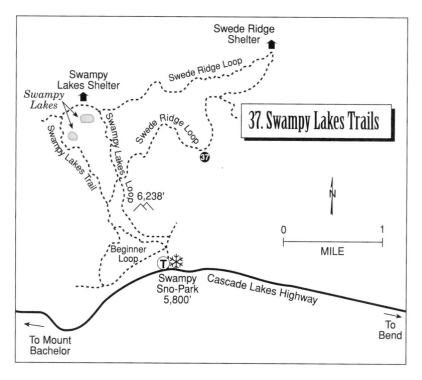

haunts to themselves. But there's no reason to disdain Swampy Lakes. It is popular, yes. But because it has so many different trail options, you can easily find a route to accommodate your needs for both exercise and wintry peace. Beginners will find at least three loops less than 2 miles long. More advanced snowshoers can fill their entire day covering trails more than 8 miles long.

Keep several tips in mind. This area historically is popular among cross-country skiers who tend to feel a little proprietary about the place. Cautiously select both your route and your actual snow track to minimize conflicts with your skiing brethren. They may quickly lose patience with snowshoers, and if you offend them enough they might think fond thoughts of banning shoers from the area. Finally, remember too that because the developed trails of Swampy Lakes frequently crisscross one another, it's easy to get the trails mixed up. An abundance of signage and traffic doesn't always help either. Your compass and the maps available at the trailhead go a long way toward helping you decipher the confusion here. Don't count on just following the signs; they can be buried under snow or otherwise obscured.

All that said, Swampy is a great place to go when the snow is fresh and you're looking for a wander in the lodgepole pine forests. There are stunning views of the Three Sisters range from several spots, most notably from the Swede Ridge Shelter.

To get to the sno-park, drive 16 miles west of Bend on the Cascade Lakes Highway. The sno-park is on the right side of the highway, just past the Virginia Meissner Sno-Park, which also has trails that access the Swampy Lakes area. You can park on either side of a forested island in the paved lot.

The easiest loop in the area is aptly named the Beginner Loop, and takes you on a 1.5-mile circuit on gentle terrain. Just follow the main Swampy Lakes Trail before turning left, or west, at the first junction you come to. The next left takes you toward the trailhead for less than a mile back to the parking lot. Most travelers head counter-clockwise on this route.

To escape the crowds, put Swede Ridge on your short list. This route scares some skiers because of its descents. As a snowshoer, you won't notice them. The Swede Ridge Shelter, built in 1995 by the Oregon National Guard Youth Challenge Program, is maintained by the Central Oregon Nordic Club. It sits above an old clear cut about 4 miles from the parking lot. From the sno-park head out on the Swampy Lakes Loop, climbing for a mile to a clear cut that holds a junction toward Swede Ridge. Go right on the Swede Ridge Loop, and for the next 2 miles trek through a lodgepole pine forest punctuated here and there with stately older fir trees. At a clear-

Swampy Lakes Trails

ing, go left toward the shelter. Start looking for the shelter below the old road in less than a mile. To get back to the trailhead, go west along the edge of another old clear cut. You can look down into Tumalo Creek Canyon from here, then dive back into the lodgepoles. In 2 miles hit the wide-open spaces of Swampy Lakes, which feature views of Mount Bachelor and Tumalo Mountain. Go left and you'll make it back to the parking lot in less than 2 miles. Go right and you'll come across the Swampy Lakes Shelter in one-eighth of a mile.

--*38*--
Tumalo Falls

Rating: Easy
Round trip: 3 miles
Starting elevation: 4,800 feet
High point: 4,800 feet
Best season: January through February
Maps: USGS Tumalo Falls
Who to contact: Deschutes National Forest, Bend/Fort Rock Ranger District, (541) 383-4000

If you're in Bend looking for a simple but extremely rewarding route, keep this one on your short list. The Tumalo Valley is beautiful in all seasons,

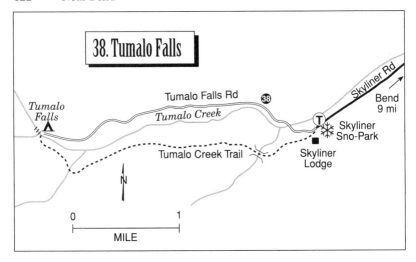

but the Tumalo Falls really show their wild beauty when surrounded by ice and snow. For some reason it's a rare year that this low valley gets enough snow, but cross your fingers and watch the forecasts.

There's been a bit of debate over just what "Tumalo" really means, but most stories point to Native Americans for the word, which has been described variously as meaning "wild plum," ground fog, or "icy creek." The latter two would apply neatly to this valley, which often features both. The Tumalo Creek drainage was the site of the 1979 Bridge Creek Fire, which still affects the vegetation here. The fire wiped out the forest that grew in the valley bottom, and you should be able to see many of the silver snags that are remnants of that conflagration. In their place is an abundance of chapparal species that cover the lower valley floor.

To get there from Bend, drive west on Galveston Street, across the Deschutes River and out of town through a quiet neighborhood. The street becomes Skyliner Road. Take this for 10 miles to get to the Skyliner Sno-Park at the end of the road.

At one point way back in central Oregon's history, this sno-park and nearby lodge were hosts to Bend's first ski area. Now it's the location for a summer science camp and the origination point for a few summer hiking trails. Park at the sno-park, walk down to the end of the road, turn right, cross Tumalo Creek on a large road bridge, and follow this road 2.5 miles up the wide, flat valley of Tumalo Creek. Stay on the north side of Tumalo Creek for the entire trip up the valley; you should see and hear the waterway at several points along the route.

The waterfalls don't announce their presence until you're right below them, but then they are a loud, crashing, dramatic bit of hydraulic action. They're impressive from below, but there are better viewpoints from the top.

Keep in mind that seemingly every year the Bend newspaper prints a story about hapless hikers falling into the waterfall. Because the best views of the falls are from the top of a steep little trail, watch your step on potentially icy and slippery slopes on the way up to the viewpoints at the top of the falls—so you don't make the front page this year. There's a massive stone parapet and wall up there, so it's relatively safe to peer down for a look.

There are two ways to return to the Skyliner Sno-Park, and both start at the campground at the base of the falls. The first is to just walk back on the road the way you came. But in those rare years when there's sufficient snow, you can also cross the creek by the campground and follow a summer biking and hiking trail back down the valley on the south side of the creek. You'll be in the brush here, but the trail is pretty new and shouldn't be too difficult to follow. When in doubt you can usually see the road and the valley from most points along the trail. The trail rolls along the contour of the hill for about 3 miles before turning downhill toward the old Skyliner Lodge. When you get to the lodge and surrounding A-frames, just walk back down the main drive toward the end of Skyliner Road.

-- 39 --
Mount Bachelor Ski Area

Rating:	Most difficult
Round trip:	3 miles
Starting elevation:	6,400 feet
High point:	9,065 feet
Best season:	November (before ski season) and May/June
Maps:	Geo-Graphics, Three Sisters Wilderness Map; USGS Broken Top
Who to contact:	Deschutes National Forest, Bend/Fort Rock Ranger District, (541) 383-4000

The top of Mount Bachelor offers unparalleled views, but you'll have to work for them by climbing more than 2,500 feet to get to the summit of this butte. Here you can get a good long look into the Three Sisters Wilderness and beyond. On a clear spring day you can see down toward Diamond Peak, to Mount Thielsen, and, I am willing to state, to Mount Shasta in California.

The critical difference between this route and almost every other trip in the book is that this hike takes place in a busy, popular ski area. Because of that, you need to take a few precautions. Tackling this route can be a bit risky, but if you're careful, abide by the rules of the ski area, and find a time to do this route without getting clobbered by skiers, it's a great hike. One of the advantages of doing a route in a ski area is that it's exceedingly difficult to get lost or wander away from civilization. The mountain is carved into ski runs, which are all labeled. You might even pick up a ski area map from the lodge or one of the many ski shops in Bend.

A word of warning: never, ever take this hike when there are skiers on the slopes. The management of the ski area will not take kindly to hordes of snowshoers clogging up the trails, even though it's public land. Use common sense. You're just not what a downhill skier or snowboarder is looking for when they're flying down the slopes of Mount Bachelor. You're also not really in a position to dodge them if they come careening at you.

Mount Bachelor Nordic Area

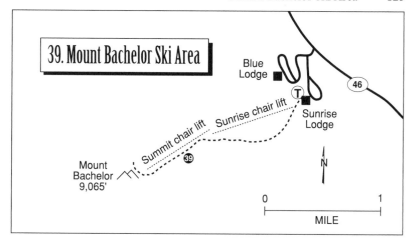

That leaves a few different windows of opportunity. In the fall, you can head for Mount Bachelor as soon as there is snow on the ground because the resort rarely opens before Thanksgiving. Or you can wait for spring and even early summer, when the days are longer. Wait until the ski area closes for the season, or hit the butte after the lifts close down, usually at 3:30 P.M. or 4 P.M. Finally, you can get up early enough to make it up and down the butte by the time the lifts open, around 8:30 A.M. or 9 A.M. Both of the pre- or postclosure options will involve a bit of snowshoeing in the dark, so bring a headlamp and warm layers. Also note that the ski patrol is not available to help you out on the slopes when the ski area is not operating.

The main parking lot for Mount Bachelor is at the end of the plowed Highway 46, but park at the Sunrise Lodge instead (because it's the more direct line to the summit). The Sunrise Lodge turnoff is 21 miles southwest of Bend and just a mile before the main lodge, almost directly across the Cascade Lakes Highway from the Dutchman Flat Sno-Park. To keep it simple, follow the major chair lift lines up to the summit. This keeps your navigational needs to a minimum—just follow the chair lift towers—but necessitates some hard, steep snowshoeing. The crampons on the bottoms of your snowshoes will come in handy here. Your calf muscles will, too. The Sunrise chair lift climbs almost directly up the hill from the lodge and you can follow it until it starts climbing steeply up a small, forested hill. You can either march straight up this hill or navigate your way on one of the ski runs to meet up with the top of this chair.

At the top of the Sunrise chair lift, you'll see the large building and base structure for the Summit chair lift off to the north. Here's your second "pitch" of the climb up Mount Bachelor. On this portion of the route you are above timberline, so watch the chair lift and if the weather turns foul, don't take any chances. If the weather is so bad that you can't follow the chair lift line, turn around. The upper portions of this route are hazardous because of the massive cirque that dominates Bachelor's upper regions. The chair lift line travels close to the edge of the cirque, and if you can't see the cornices, it's not smart to proceed.

In good weather, climb up the southern ridge of the Summit chair lift area; there are stunning views all around you, and the trail is wide and flat and, if in season, well groomed. The top of the chair lift is about as high as you want to go. You're not quite at Bachelor's summit, but the higher reaches can be treacherous. Often a good bit of rime ice builds up at the top of Bachelor, and a poor snowshoe placement can send you tumbling. The views to the south actually are best from the top of the chair lift. To view the Three Sisters Wilderness, look back the way you came.

--40--
Broken Top

Rating: Backcountry
Round trip: 10 miles
Starting elevation: 6,400 feet
High point: 6,900 feet
Best season: December through June
Maps: Geo-Graphics, Three Sisters Wilderness Map; USGS Broken Top
Who to contact: Deschutes National Forest, Bend/Fort Rock Ranger District, (541) 383-4000

It's a long but utterly beautiful haul into the crater area of Broken Top, and it's worth every step. Oregon's mountains are formed almost exclusively by volcanic action, and getting a close look at Broken Top reveals just how severe that action was. This hike gives you a close-up view of the crater of the blasted-out mountain. The closer you get to the gaping maw of Broken Top, the more impressive it gets. It only gets bigger, and you only feel smaller, when you stand in front of this example of volatile volcanism. The craggy skyline of the summit of Broken Top is unmistakable from any perspective, especially when it's surrounded by the more composed summits of The Three Sisters.

The crater's interior is filled with glaciers that hang precariously from

Broken Top

the vertical interior walls. By the time you get to Broken Top, you'll be well past timberline, and the dense forests of the central Cascades give way to the wide-open spaces of the Three Sisters alpine country.

There are several ways to get to Broken Top in the winter, but shooting across from the Dutchman Flat Sno-Park is the most direct route. You'll cross through several different busy areas, including immaculate cross-country ski trails, rutted-out snowmobile tracks, and the sort of unmarked woods that all good snowshoers relish.

To get there from Bend, drive 20 miles southwest on the Cascades Lakes Highway/Highway 46 until you reach the Dutchman Flat Sno-Park. On weekends be prepared for crowds of nordic skiers and snowmobilers. On this trip you'll encounter all manner of winter traveler, so grin and bear the crowds for a little while.

Follow the Big Meadow Trail out of the Dutchman Flat trail network. That means you should walk out across the Dutchman Flat toward the Water Tower Trail until you reach the Big Meadow Trail. Head toward Todd Lake, but when you get to the Big Meadow itself, cross Forest Road 370. From here there are two ways to go. One is to go straight after you cross the road and walk through the trees and into a large meadow. The other is to just walk up Forest Road 370, a snowmobile route, until it crosses the Crater Creek Ditch, which is a more prominent feature than you might think. Another useful landmark is Moon Mountain, a low but distinctive hump

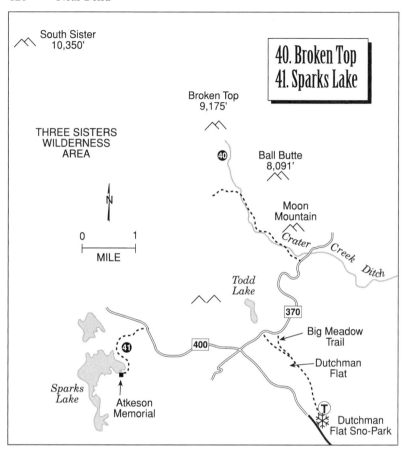

South Sister
10,350'

40. Broken Top
41. Sparks Lake

Broken Top
9,175'

THREE SISTERS
WILDERNESS
AREA

40

Ball Butte
8,091'

Moon
Mountain

Crater *Creek*
Ditch

N

0   1
MILE

Todd
Lake

370

Big Meadow
Trail

400

41

Dutchman
Flat

Sparks
Lake

Atkeson
Memorial

T

Dutchman
Flat Sno-Park

that you want to keep on your north shoulder. From here you head out into the wide apron of the lower crater, and—in good weather—you should be able to see where you're going. You can still follow the Crater Creek Ditch right up to the base of the crater. Believe me, you'll know when you're there.

Something to remember, though, is that the sides of the crater's interior are far from stable in midwinter, and in spring they can release wet slides and even rocks. The closer you get, the more you can see that the interior of Broken Top is littered with the rotten lava rock that forms this craggy peak, stuff that's fallen from the heights of the crater rim to the floor of the crater.

Soon after you leave the forest road and snowmobile track, you cross into the Three Sisters Wilderness. In fact, you may encounter the weathered wooden sign that marks the wilderness boundary. But it's an imperfect boundary line, something that doesn't always seem clear to everyone. So don't be surprised if you see snowmobilers riding closer than you think they should be.

The base of the crater gets heavy, blazing sun in the springtime and there's little shade from trees up here. Depending on the temperature, the sun may be a welcome sight, but don't get caught without some form of sun protection.

--*41*--
Sparks Lake

Rating:	Most difficult
Round trip:	10 miles
Starting elevation:	6,400 feet
High point:	6,400 feet
Best season:	December through April
Maps:	Geo-Graphics, Three Sisters Wilderness Map; USGS South Sister; USGS Broken Top
Who to contact:	Deschutes National Forest, Bend/Fort Rock Ranger District, (541) 388-5446

This may be the prettiest road-based tour in the Bend area. It's a long way down the hill to this lake and back, but traveling on the road is relatively straightforward. So despite the distance, this is a tour that any intermediate snowshoer in good shape can tackle. Sparks Lake is an excellent viewpoint to take in the wide sweep of the Three Sisters region, and the mellow terrain along the road makes for easy gawking along the way. Bring a camera to capture the sublime mountain views. In fact, there is a spot on this lakeshore with a small memorial to Ray Atkeson, a celebrated Oregon photographer who took amazing photos of this area.

The high point here is also your starting point. From the Dutchman Flat Sno-Park it's almost an even 1,000-foot drop to the wide lake basin, which sits at 5,428 feet. The elevation loss and gain happens over a few miles, so there's not much steep climbing to do here. It is, however, a long, steady march out of the lake basin and back up to the Dutchman Flat area.

The Dutchman Flat Sno-Park is located 21 miles southwest of Bend on the Cascade Lakes Highway/Highway 46. This highway is closed early in the winter; it's the same road that you'll be hiking on as you make your way down to Sparks Lake. Be aware that this is a snowmobile route that

On the road to Sparks Lake

gets a bit of traffic on winter weekends. But even then, the road is so wide that you'll be able to see and hear them coming long before they get to you. Still, to avoid confusion, make sure you stay to the side of the trail when snowmobiles come your way.

For the first 2 miles, you pass through relatively open meadows. The trails of the Mount Bachelor Nordic Ski Area are to the left and right here. In less than 2 miles come across Forest Road 370, the Todd Lake access road. Keep on keeping on here, past Forest Road 370 and some substantial cliffs and knobs to the north of the road. These hills hide the Todd Lake Basin, barely a mile away from where you're hiking.

But the Todd Lake Basin Trail is for another day. Proceed onward here and see meadows, snow-covered swamps, and mixed forest off to the south of the road. There's also a small, unnamed knob to the south just after you pass the Todd Lake junction.

Sparks Lake is down a long, wide hill from the Todd Lake junction. You can't miss the massive, sprawling basin of Sparks Lake, which sits off to the south and west of the road. After you drop the 1,000 feet off of the hill from Dutchman Flat and the Todd Lake junction, Sparks Lake becomes evident first as a wide swampy meadow. If you keep hiking, just over 2 miles from the Todd Lake junction is an access road to the Sparks Lake area. The road, Forest Road 400, also accesses the Soda Creek Campground. Disregard the campground and make the extra 1-mile trek to the lakeshore and a brilliant view of Mount Bachelor. Anybody who's ever purchased a Ray Atkeson book or calendar should recognize this viewpoint. All around you here are wide swamps around the edge of the lake. In another half mile come to the small picnic area near a peninsula, where you get marvelous views of the surrounding mountains, meadows, and wilderness. To return, simply follow the road back toward the ski area.

--*42*--
Edison Butte—AC/DC Shelter

Rating: More difficult
Round trip: 5.7 miles
Starting elevation: 5,080 feet
High point: 5,620 feet
Best season: December to March
Maps: USFS Deschutes National Forest; USGS Wanoga Butte
Who to contact: Deschutes National Forest, Bend/Fort Rock Ranger District, (541) 383-4000

The Edison Butte Trails are relatively recent additions to the already dense central Oregon trails network. But you'll soon see why locals love them. For one, they take pressure off of the busy trails around Swampy Lakes and Dutchman Flat. For another, they offer a wide range of possibilities for short and long loops alike.

The name of this trail is sure to highlight some generational differences among snowshoers. Older readers will make the connection to Thomas Edison and his electrical discoveries, and those born recently enough to sample the early days of heavy metal rock music might think of a certain hard-driving metal band. Sorry, young ones, you're out of luck here.

Although the name might confuse some readers, the AC/DC Shelter is a

AC/DC Shelter

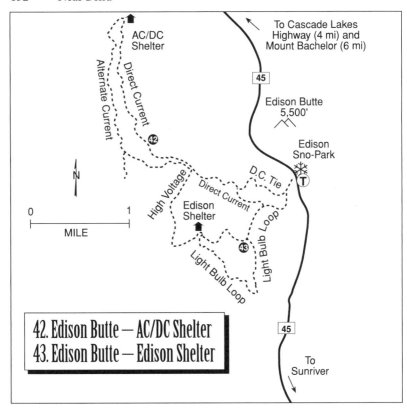

To Cascade Lakes
Highway (4 mi) and
Mount Bachelor (6 mi)

AC/DC
Shelter

Alternate Current

Direct Current

45

Edison Butte
5,500'

Edison
Sno-Park

T

D.C. Tie

42

Direct Current

High Voltage

Edison
Shelter

Light Bulb Loop

43

N

0   1

MILE

Light Bulb Loop

42. Edison Butte – AC/DC Shelter
43. Edison Butte – Edison Shelter

45

To
Sunriver

welcome spot for a rest, located in a serene and quiet mountain meadow. This is one of those routes that's a lot of fun after fresh snow, since it never climbs all that steeply, and the trail's undulations make for interesting climbing and descending. The Edison Butte Trails are an intriguing spider web of trails that weave in and out of some beautiful subalpine forest. In these trails you can find stately ponderosa pine, with their brilliantly contrasting yellow-orange bark, and the scraggly boughs of mountain hemlock and lodgepole pine.

The Edison Butte Sno-Park is located just 4 miles down Road 45 from the Cascade Lakes Highway/Highway 46. The turnoff is about 18 miles southwest of Bend and is the same route Sunriver residents and guests use to get back and forth from the Mount Bachelor Ski Area. So be aware that there will be traffic, but not all of it headed to your snowshoeing destination. There are two sections of the Edison Butte parking lot. Snowmobilers dominate half of the lot, as this area serves as an operations base for snowmobile roads that, fortunately, do not cross many of the Edison Butte ski and snowshoe trails.

The AC/DC Shelter is at the top of the Direct Current Trail, a rolling trail that climbs 600 feet in less than 3 miles. From the parking lot's southern end, follow the trail west, taking the first right-hand turn. In about a half mile cross one of the snowmobile routes, where you should be aware that snow machines can come up quicker than you might think.

At the 1-mile mark, another junction presents itself. A left here takes you to the Edison Butte Shelter. Instead go right to reach the AC/DC Shelter in 1.5 miles. The trail here is a steady uphill climb through ever-denser forests. At the junction along the way, bear right.

The shelter itself is one of those well-built structures with a fully functioning wood stove and, in most years, a good supply of firewood. It's located in a wide, flat meadow at the base of a small hill. The shelter is tucked into a corner of the meadow and, in heavy snow years, you might have to climb down into the doorway.

There is some talk of building a trail from the AC/DC Shelter to the Vista Butte Sno-Park area, but currently there's nothing more than a word-of-mouth route there. Instead, walk past the shelter, across the meadow, and down the Alternate Current Trail, which drops you out at the sno-park again in about 3 miles. On the way back, follow much of the same trails you used on the way up, but make sure to bear left at most junctions to get back to the sno-park.

Outcrop on the Edison Butte Trail

--*43*--
Edison Butte—Edison Shelter

Rating: Easy
Round trip: 3.5 miles
Starting elevation: 5,080 feet
High point: 5,100 feet
Best season: January through March
Maps: USFS Deschutes National Forest; USGS Wanoga Butte
Who to contact: Deschutes National Forest, Bend/Fort Rock Ranger District, (541) 383-4000

This is one of the short (you can do it in about 2 hours), fun, and easy loop trails among the Edison Butte area's veritable spaghetti-noodle pile of trails that crisscross each other through dense forests of ponderosa and lodgepole pine. The Edison Butte area is a newer addition to central Oregon's winter trails bounty, and the diversity of trails and routes here are well appreciated by skiers and 'shoers alike. The trails are all well marked and easy to follow, with occasional head-scratching induced by the multiple trail junctions. Keep your cool, however, and you'll get a fun day out of twisting and turning through the forest.

To get to the sno-park, drive 18 miles southwest of Bend on the Cascade Lakes Highway/Highway 46, toward Mount Bachelor. Turn off on Road 45 toward Sunriver, and drive 4 miles south to the Edison Butte Sno-Park. From Sunriver it's just over 12 miles to the Edison Butte Sno-Park. The Edison Shelter is accessed via the Light Bulb Loop (all the trail names here make reference to Thomas Edison's work with electricity) and offers a mellow walk through the winter woods. The trailhead for the Edison Shelter is at the eastern end of the parking lot. You'll notice that you're sharing the parking lot with snowmobilers. They love this area, but fortunately they're barred from most routes that snowshoers and skiers use.

From the trailhead, walk less than a quarter mile to the first junction. Take a left here and notice the blue diamonds on the trees, which make following the trail a relatively simple affair.

After this first junction, pass through a beautiful stand of older ponderosa pine and get a sense of why the older trees are sometimes referred to as "Yellowbellies" by foresters. Pass straight through this little grove toward the second junction at the half-mile mark. Turn left here and wander through a scruffier forest of lodgepole pine. In another half mile, turn south or right toward the shelter.

The shelter itself is up on a hilltop, which on a clear day can offer decent views of surrounding territory. Because the Edison Butte trail network only opened in 1987, this shelter isn't exactly "rustic," but it does sport a great porch to sit on during inclement weather. The cabin is maintained by the Central Oregon Nordic Club, whose members ask visitors not to use it as an overnight shelter. That said, it's hard not to linger for a while over lunch.

From the shelter go directly west, where you can pick up the other half of the Light Bulb Loop. It's just 2 miles back to the sno-park from here. If you find yourself wandering past a sunken cave, you've probably discovered the Edison Ice Caves, a local landmark that is shrouded in mystery only because authorities don't want to disturb a population of Townsend long-eared bats that live in the cave. The Townsend is an endangered species and should be given plenty of elbow room. That means stay out of the cave. A proposed snowmobile route past the cave was nixed in order to protect the bat population.

And although dogs are allowed, you're discouraged from bringing them here because of the popularity of the area and the potential for your furry friends to leave land mines for others to grumble over. Dogs also have a tendency—like snowshoers—to destroy a good ski track.

Old ponderosa at Edison Butte

--44--
South Sister

Rating: Most difficult/backcountry
Round trip: 10 miles from Devils Lake Campground
Starting elevation: 5,400 feet at Devils Lake Campground
High point: 10,358 feet
Best season: May through July
Maps: Geo-Graphics, Three Sisters Wilderness Map; USGS South Sister
Who to contact: Deschutes National Forest, Bend/Fort Rock Ranger District, (541) 383-4000

Here's a test of your quadriceps. This potentially grueling climb up the southernmost peak in the Three Sisters Wilderness is a great springtime snowshoe outing. From the summit of South Sister you've got the astounding reach of the Three Sisters Wilderness before you, as well as views north almost to Mount Hood, and south almost to Mount Shasta. The summit of South Sister is host to a dramatic teardrop lake that forms out of a depression filled with ice for much of the year. The climb up the peak leads you past yawning glaciers and dramatic fields of cooled lava.

You're likely to see other mountaineering enthusiasts here, some with skis or snowboards, but don't feel like you need special equipment to climb this mountain. Certainly, every precaution about avalanche hazard applies here. Preparation for this trip should include snow shovels, avalanche beacons, and some avalanche safety know-how. You'll also need to be well-versed in map and compass use for this trip, which wastes no time in getting

Broken Top and the moon

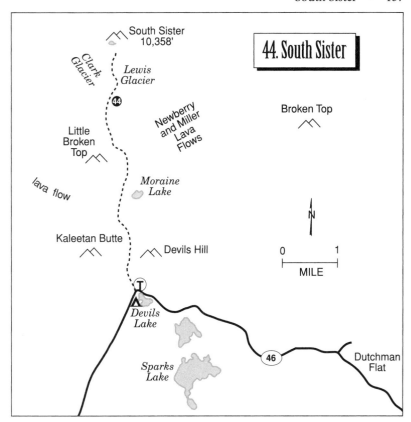

44. South Sister

South Sister 10,358'

Clark Glacier

Lewis Glacier

44

Newberry and Miller Lava Flows

Broken Top

Little Broken Top

lava flow

Moraine Lake

Kaleetan Butte

Devils Hill

N

0   1
MILE

Devils Lake

Sparks Lake

46

Dutchman Flat

way, way off the beaten path. Having an altimeter isn't a bad idea for this route, either. And, although you might encounter backcountry skiers or snowboarders here, you can't necessarily count on their tracks to lead you to the summit because they're not always headed there.

To get there from Bend, take the Cascade Lakes Highway/Highway 46 for 27 miles, past Mount Bachelor toward the Devils Lake Campground. To do this route in the winter, when the Cascade Lakes Highway is closed off at the Dutchman Flat Sno-Park, would add an extra 5 miles of road each way to the bargain. Waiting until you can drive to the Devils Lake Campground maximizes your time on the mountain, something well worth the wait until spring.

The Devils Lake Campground is 5 miles from the open snow gate just past Dutchman Flat. The parking lot is on the south side of the highway, but you'll hike on the north side of the road. Climb straight up the Hell Creek drainage, which can be steep at times. There's a definite cleft in the rim to the Wickiup Plains, where the route goes between Devils Hill and Kaleetan Butte. Pop out onto a rim and the tree cover, which had been very dense, will thin out dramatically. If you go too far to the east after topping out of the Hells Creek drainage, you'll encounter Moraine Lake. Instead push north across the rim of a plateau above the lake. This wide shelf crosses beneath a small peak called Little Broken Top for reasons that will be obvious once you get a look at it. Off to the right are the Newberry and Miller Lava Flows, and to the left, or west, is the Rock Mesa Obsidian Flow. Even with snow cover these lava flows are distinguishable from the rest of the mountainous landscape.

Above Little Broken Top, two prominent glaciers will appear above you. Follow the obvious ridge that climbs up from the Moraine Lake plateau. This route climbs to a saddle at 9,000 feet, right below the Lewis Glacier. Here you can find another depression in the mountain that in the summer becomes another teardrop lake. The route to the top should be obvious now; follow the ridge and take care not to travel out onto the Lewis Glacier to the east or the Clark Glacier to the south. Both are ridden with crevasses and dangerous to inexperienced alpinists.

The last 1,300 feet of climbing are straightforward, unrelenting, and steep. The summit of South Sister is really at the northern end of the rim, but the huge craterlike depression in the top of this mountain may feel close enough for tired legs.

--45--
Sisters Traverse

Rating: Backcountry/most difficult
Round trip: Approximately 30 miles
Starting elevation: 6,400 feet
High point: 6,500 feet
Best season: January through June
Maps: Geo-Graphics, Three Sisters Wilderness Map; USGS South Sister
Who to contact: Deschutes National Forest, Bend/Fort Rock Ranger District, (541) 383-4000; or Willamette National Forest, McKenzie Ranger District, (541) 822-3381

This is a major achievement for accomplished snowshoers, and a trip you'll remember for a long time. The solitude and wilderness experience that

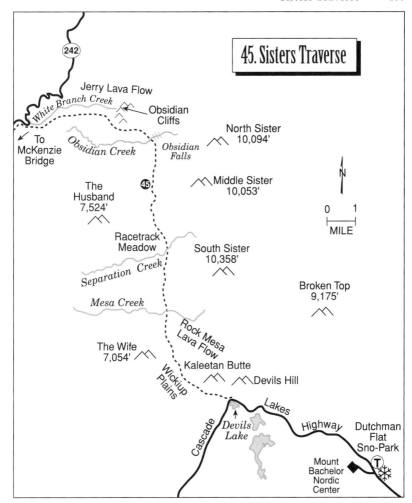

45. Sisters Traverse

you get out of a Three Sisters traverse is astounding. You just won't see many people wandering this deep in the winter woods. There are high lake basins, craggy passes, deep forest creeks, and some of the most substantial groves of subalpine old-growth forest I've ever seen. Some of the trees on this route are massive, an amazing accomplishment at this altitude, so close to timberline.

This route is also, bar none, the hardest trip in this book. It will definitely challenge your backcountry know-how. At the start of the route the access to the Wickiup Plains isn't well marked and you'll be doing some

North Sister

bushwacking before you get to the high country, but it actually gets easier as you go on. Once you get up on the apron of the Three Sisters mountains, you'll be marching steadily along high subalpine environments with jaw-dropping views of surrounding peaks. This route requires a shuttle. I recommend snowshoeing from the Dutchman Flat Sno-Park north to the Old McKenzie Highway, Forest Road 242. During winter, park a car near the White Branch Youth Camp, in front of a snow gate. Come out of the woods near Alder Springs, where the White Branch Creek flows toward the highway.

There is no well-marked or frequently traveled trail here. You will be more or less tracking the Pacific Crest National Scenic Trail, but it won't be visible and, to preserve the wilderness character of this area, there are few marks on trees to guide you. I'll describe landmarks that you can use to make your own way across this wilderness area (listing every twist and turn would require a separate book). On this serious route it's absolutely essential that you carry a map, compass, and altimeter if you can get one. It's easy to get lost out here if the weather turns foul and the Sisters disappear from view. Even with these dramatic mountains in your sight, watch your path carefully to make sure you stay on the right elevation and contour.

If it's possible, given the weather, try to skirt the edge of timberline once you get past the Wickiup Plains. This makes navigation easier, and you avoid plunging too deep into creeks and canyons. But although the easiest traveling is done above tree line, this is also the zone where you're likely to encounter cornices formed by blowing snow. In flat light you can just about walk off the edge of a cornice without even noticing—until it's too late.

You can do this route in midwinter, but waiting until February, March, or even later will give you better weather and longer days. In fact, if you do this route as late as May or June, you can cut off some of the road time on either end, but you do risk encountering thin snow.

To get to the trip's starting point from Bend, drive 21 miles southwest on the Cascade Lakes Highway/Highway 46 to the Dutchman Flat Sno-Park. From Dutchman Flat, head to the Devils Lake Campground on the snowed-over and closed-off Cascade Lakes Highway. It's almost 6 miles to this spot alone, so consider looking for a campground somewhere up on the Wickiup Plains, another 2 miles. Turn into the woods at Devils Lake, but don't head up toward Moraine Lake. Instead traverse around the west side of Kaleetan Butte and access the Wickiup Plains at the base of the Rock Mesa Lava Flow. Getting to the plains puts you up onto the elevation level you'll be traveling for much of the trip, and gets you out of the tight woods below and into the dramatic subalpine country. This isn't a bad spot for a first night's rest.

From the Wickiup Plains start to see first The Wife and then The Husband appear. These smaller peaks are useful navigational points from which to take compass bearings in order to triangulate your position on the route. The Wife is a smaller peak to the west of the Rock Mesa Lava Flow, and The Husband is a 7,524-foot peak that sits to the west just between the South and Middle Sisters.

Several streams cross this route and most of them flow down off the glaciers of the Three Sisters. Depending on the snow conditions, some of these creeks can make for tricky crossing, while others narrow to a trickle and are well covered by snow. If you push from the Rock Mesa Lava Flow to Obsidian Falls in one day, it's a long but doable haul of about 10 miles of travel. You can make this route short but grueling by doing it that way, or you can choose to camp above Racetrack Meadow or on one of the small benches to the southwest of Middle Sister. Either way, if you are going to make the push from Obsidian Falls down the Jerry Lava Flow to the highway and out, that's a long day in and of itself.

Don't think that getting to Highway 242 means the trip is over. Hiking from the wilderness boundary down to the parking area still takes some doing. Also, be aware that the Obsidian Cliffs are a significant hazard; you can contour around them relatively easily and still follow the White Branch down to the highway. The southern tributary of White Branch Creek flows out of Sister Springs, near Obsidian Falls, and can be another useful route to follow out.

By now you should recognize that there is no right or wrong way to do this trip. Weather, snow conditions, and your own abilities and ambitions will change the nature of this adventure. I recommend camping when possible, instead of killing yourself just to make a lot of miles. Remember that you're out here to enjoy yourself, not just to motor through the woods. It's an incredible place to spend as many days as you can manage.

--46--
Todd Lake

Rating: More difficult
Round trip: 6.5 miles
Starting elevation: 6,300 feet
High point: 6,300 feet
Best season: December through March
Maps: Geo-Graphics, Three Sisters Wilderness Map;
USFS Deschutes National Forest
Who to contact: Deschutes National Forest, Bend/Fort Rock Ranger
District, (541) 383-4000

This well-hidden gem of a lake is well worth the routefinding it might take to get to it. You'll find Todd Lake tucked neatly away in a deep, wide basin. Because it's off the outer ring of cross-country ski and snowshoe trails that radiate out from Dutchman Flats, it's also not as heavily traveled as the trails around it. You're well insulated from snowmobile noise—or any kind of noise for that matter.

There are two places to start this hike: Dutchman Flat Sno-Park or the Mount Bachelor Nordic Center. To get there from Bend, take the Cascade Lakes Highway/Highway 46 for 21 miles southwest to the Dutchman Flat Sno-Park. The Mount Bachelor Nordic Center is a little more than a mile farther up the road. The sno-park is usually clogged with snowmobilers on winter weekends, so start from the nordic center. The modest cabin at the nordic center houses a small store, rental shop, and information center that is staffed during the regular ski season. Here you can inquire inside about route information and snow conditions. Be aware that this area began as a cross-country skier's resort, and the trails are groomed primarily for that use. There's always room on the trail for snowshoers and skiers alike, but be careful not to disturb the tracks that are set for skiers.

From the nordic center take the Mount Bachelor Common Corridor across the snowed-over Cascade Lakes Highway, which in winter is a snowmobiler's thoroughfare. The Todd Lake Trail starts across the road and immediately plunges into a dense but beautiful forest that shifts between lodgepole pine and older mountain hemlock. Soon you will find yourself walking along the edge of a wide meadow to your left, with a short ridge to your right.

The trail descends gently here, paralleling the Cascade Lakes Highway toward the summertime access road to Todd Lake, Forest Road 370. Cross several junctions, the first being a junction with the Water Tower Trail. Stay to the left and travel west here. Eventually the Todd Lake Trail winds

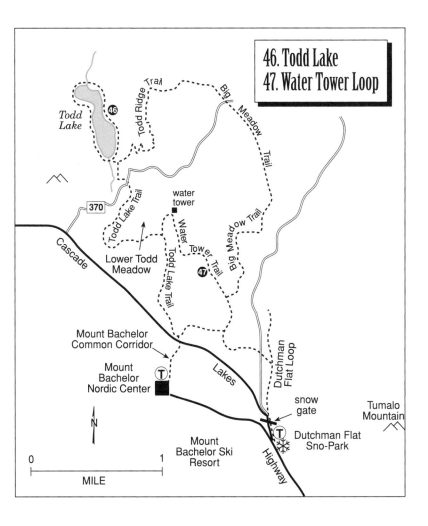

to the north and away from the Cascade Lakes Highway, and through a bit of forest. Shortly thereafter, however, the trail crosses another meadow, called Lower Todd Meadow. Yes, that means you're getting very close. Continue north through the meadow, and cross Road 370, watching for speeding snowmobilers. Across the road is a lake access road that leads past a snow gate, through a small picnic ground, and to the lake's southwestern shores.

It's absolutely worth your while to do the short loop hike around the lake. Most folks go counterclockwise, and if the sun is out the nearest eastern shores get the bulk of it. Take your lunch break here. Like every Oregon lake, this one looks frozen solid in the winter, but don't push it by walking out onto the lake's center. On the northern side of the lake, the wide basin walls are all that separates you from the high plains in front of Broken Top. There's also a campground on the northwestern side of the lake that's accessible only by foot—even in the summertime. During the winter you would be hard-pressed to locate it. If you do opt to climb to the top of the ridges surrounding the lake basin, choose the northernmost ridge. The angle is easier to climb and isn't as prone to avalanches as the eastern or western sides might be. Either way, be aware that if the conditions are right, an avalanche could occur on the lake basin walls.

--47--
Water Tower Loop

Rating: Easy
Round trip: 2.5 miles
Starting elevation: 6,400 feet
High point: 6,400 feet
Best season: December through March
Maps: Geo-Graphics, Three Sisters Wilderness Map;
USFS Deschutes National Forest
Who to contact: Deschutes National Forest, Bend/Fort Rock Ranger
District, (541) 383-4000

The forests between the Dutchman Flat and Todd Lake are a beautiful example of the mixed-species woods in central Oregon. This short loop leads you through dense groves of lodgepole pine mixed with statuesque, ancient mountain hemlock—a beautiful sample of central Oregon's forests.

The Water Tower Loop is one of those trails with a name that actually makes some sense; you will, in fact, pass an old water tower at the foot of a beautiful, wide meadow. The old hulk of steel and iron isn't much to look at, but the tower itself serves as a handy landmark for skiers and snowshoers who are out wandering these woods and makes a fine objective for an afternoon's walk through the forest. You won't, of course, be the first person to travel this way, and that comes with advantages and disadvantages. The route is well signed and intersects several popular trails (though I've never seen these trails actually crowded). You won't be alone on all but the snowiest weekdays, but you also won't have to work too hard to stay on track, either. That's an advantage for novice routefinders. Still, you should take a map with you; the many junctions can make this route confusing. Be aware that all roads definitely do not lead to Rome; plan your route well and take the correct turns as indicated on the signs and your maps, or you'll end up on a much more ambitious outing than you may have bargained for.

Start from the Dutchman Flat Sno-Park, which is on the Cascade Lakes Highway/Highway 46 between the two entrances to the Mount Bachelor Ski Resort. The turnoff is about 21 miles southwest of Bend. You'll start at the foot of Tumalo Mountain, an elevation of about 6,250 feet.

From the sno-park strike out across Dutchman Flat on the Dutchman Loop Trail; stay to the right and skirt the base of Tumalo Mountain. (This puts you at the edge of the forest and not out in the middle of the meadow

Water Tower Loop

where snowmobilers track up the open areas.) This is the heaviest use area of the trail. Make your first left on the Dutchman Flat Loop trail and cross the meadow. At the next junction you intersect with the Todd Lake Trail. Stay to the right here, and begin to enter the woods.

When you come to a junction with the Big Meadow Trail, turn left. As you trek deeper into the woods, keep an eye out for the larger specimens of mountain hemlock. In this section of the woods you'll come across a couple of short, somewhat steep sections. Watch out for nordic skiers who may or may not be in control of their skis as they descend this trail. Skiers often have to negotiate a lot of smaller undergrowth trees as they careen downhill. It's your turn to be gracious here and step aside.

The mighty water tower itself sits at the opposite end of a small meadow, just in the edge of the trees. Be aware that several trails head out from this meadow to points beyond. There's a junction here for Little Meadow and Big Meadow to the right, and if you go straight and to the west, you'll drop down toward Forest Road 370, the Todd Lake access road.

To avoid confusion, however, just backtrack your route to the tower. Other routes back to the Dutchman Flat Sno-Park would require more miles and more routefinding. Judge your group's abilities and stamina before you decide which route to take for your return. Be aware, too, that a creek borders the meadow at one end and is partially hidden by the deep snows of late winter. They may be snow-covered, but as often as not the water is still flowing beneath the snow.

--48--
Vista Butte

> **Rating:** More difficult
> **Round trip:** 4.5 miles
> **Starting elevation:** 5,900 feet
> **High point:** 6,619 feet
> **Best season:** January through March
> **Maps:** Geo-Graphics, Three Sisters Wilderness Map; USGS Wanoga Butte
> **Who to contact:** Deschutes National Forest, Bend/Fort Rock Ranger District, (541) 383-4000

It's not called Vista Butte for nothing: the views from atop this humble backwoods knob are indeed stunning. This route showcases the local moun-

Mount Bachelor from Vista Butte

tains, and the sparse lodgepole pine forest makes for easy walking, even in the woods. From atop Vista Butte you can easily blow several frames of film; the panorama of central Oregon backcountry spreads out nicely before you. The location and elevation of this little knob are just enough to allow for miraculous views in all directions. You can look down on the Swampy Lakes area and its trails to the south; Bachelor Butte and the Bach-

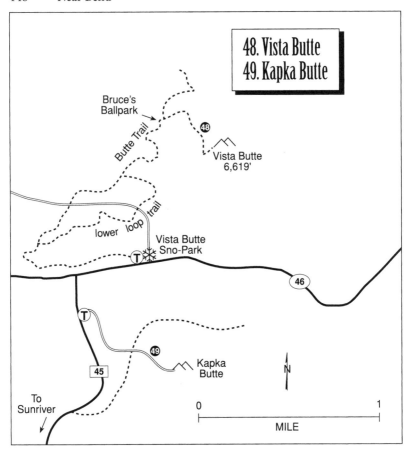

48. Vista Butte
49. Kapka Butte

Bruce's Ballpark

Butte Trail

48

Vista Butte
6,619'

lower loop trail

Vista Butte
Sno-Park

46

45

49

Kapka
Butte

N

To
Sunriver

0   1

MILE

elor ski area to the north; and Broken Top and the Three Sisters mountains to the east.

Also, it's not a very long haul to the top of the butte from the Vista Butte Sno-Park. This route is feasible for most beginner snowshoers who are in decent physical condition. You won't gain much elevation here, and forgiving switchbacks help you along the few steady uphill climbs.

The Vista Butte Sno-Park is really nothing more than a wide spot on the Cascade Lakes Highway/Highway 46, about 16 miles southwest of Bend, and just before the turnoff to Sunriver. The turnoff itself is on the north side of the highway. The trail begins right off the road.

For the first quarter mile or so the trail parallels the highway. After a short while, come even with the Sunriver highway junction. Soon after this point, follow the trail as it switchbacks; you now begin climbing in earnest.

At the half-mile mark, see a junction for the lower loop trail, which you might choose to take if you're looking for a less-steep route to the top. The left turn is more direct. The lower and upper trails meet a little farther up. Also, from about this junction you might begin to see Vista Butte, rising from the forest. From your vantage point it's a low forested hump, and you've got about 480 feet of elevation to gain. You also might see a snowmobile track here at the end of the meadow. You can avoid that track by taking the right turn for the lower loop trail. After a while you will come alongside an east–west snowmobile track. This is one of those tight woodsy snowmobile trails that, for some reason, snowmobilers feel a need to diverge from. Therefore, be careful crossing the track, because you can't depend on snowmobilers to stay on it.

After another bit of hiking, at the 1.75-mile mark, come to the junction with the Butte Trail to the top. Take the left junction. At elevation 6,460 feet, notice the sign for Bruce's Ballpark. As far as I can tell, the only reason to call it that is because of the good echoes you might be able to throw.

Climb the gentle but steady uphill grade a bit farther to the summit. In all but the worst weather, it's obvious when you're at the summit.

--49--
Kapka Butte

Rating:	Easy/backcountry
Round trip:	2 miles
Starting elevation:	5,900 feet
High point:	6,170 feet
Best season:	January through March
Maps:	Geo-Graphics, Three Sisters Wilderness Map; USGS Wanoga Butte
Who to contact:	Deschutes National Forest, Bend/Fort Rock Ranger District, (541) 383-4000

Lousy ski day? Need to stretch your legs a bit? Looking for a quick, good view? Head for Kapka Butte, which is the shortest route to earn a "backcountry" rating in this book. This route lacks a trail, summer or winter, to the summit. But don't let that deter you; take a compass and start walking. The summit of Kapka offers excellent views—all the way into northern California on a good day. You're sufficiently west of Bachelor Butte that you can see around the big hill. That's where Shasta comes into view when all things work out right.

This may be a bit of an "outlaw" trip, because there aren't any trails and there's hardly even a parking area. But it's such a great short march to the top of this butte that I felt I had to include it here. The summit area of Kapka Butte features beautiful and massive ponderosa pines. Here you can discover why old-timers and Oregon pioneers referred to this tree species as the "Yellowbelly" pine. As the pine ages, the bark adopts a lighter color. Ancient ponderosa pine trees are indeed just about yellow in color. The bark arranges itself into massive plates around the girth of the tree. They grow much taller than most lodgepole pine trees, and their long needles are distinctive even at a great distance.

To get to Kapka, you can first try to park at a wide spot on Forest Road 45, which turns off from the Cascade Lakes Highway/Highway 46 between Bend and the Mount Bachelor Ski Area. The turnoff is about 16 miles southwest of Bend. After turning off from the Cascade Lakes Highway, you can try to park at a wide spot in the road just one-tenth of a mile away from the Cascade Lakes Highway. This is not a sno-park, so if the road is snowy or otherwise inhospitable for parking, consider parking at the Vista Butte Sno-Park back on the Cascade Lakes Highway and walking down to this point.

Either way, from Road 45 you can enter the woods and follow an old road cut between the trees that parallels Road 45 going south. Kapka Butte is the small hill to your left, or to the east of Road 45.

A snowmobile trail passes by Kapka Butte at the base of the road. Hike less than a quarter mile down the old road cut before turning due east and marching toward the hill. Cross the snowmobile tracks (watching out for flying snowmobilers as you do) and begin to head up the hill. Here's where a compass becomes handy, because you're no longer following any trail.

Once upon the sides of Kapka Butte, you'll almost immediately begin to pass by the larger ponderosa pines. If you stay on the western side of the butte, you'll get better views, and in late spring the sun stays on this aspect the longest. Pick your way up the hill based on the path of least resistance. Expect to hit small thickets of younger trees and downed logs here. Don't expect smooth sailing on a groomed path. That's not what this route is about.

The summit of Kapka Butte doesn't announce itself with grand rocky outcroppings. Instead, you'll notice the hill leveling out. Stay on the western edge of the "summit" of Kapka because, again, that will get you in line for the best views. Mount Bachelor is right in your face; you can't miss it—except on a lousy day. Tumalo Mountain is across the highway. Notice its dramatically barren eastern face, which in the winter can develop a large cornice that is visible from this vantage point. If you're lucky and the weather is clear, you might make out a distant white triangle. That's Mount Shasta in northern California, seen from atop this tiny but lovely little hill.

--*50*--
Black Butte

Rating:	Most difficult
Round trip:	10 miles
Starting elevation:	4,000 feet
High point:	6,400 feet
Best season:	January through February
Maps:	USGS Black Butte
Who to contact:	Deschutes National Forest, Sisters Ranger District, (541) 549-7700

Black Butte is known for being almost perfectly conical in form. Of course, the closer you get to the summit, the less this will seem like the case, but from a distance the central Oregon landmark cuts a striking figure in the skyline. In the winter it receives few visitors, but don't let this stop you. There's

Black Butte area

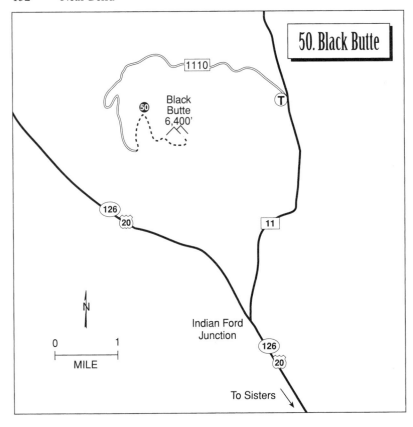

a lot to see from its summit, and getting to the top is a good test of your stamina.

The summit of this imposing landmark is a great spot for central Oregon views in all directions. There's the added benefit of seeing Black Butte as you drive back and forth between the Willamette Valley and the Bend and Sisters area, which means that, if you successfully attain the summit, you can sigh with satisfaction as this hill's massive bulk comes into view. It's not an easy climb, even though it looks like it should be, but it's worth the effort.

There are really two ways to climb Black Butte. The first way, which will be described here as the preferred method, is to follow the road to the summit. The second, which is more direct but possibly more frustrating, is to point your snowshoes at the summit and start climbing.

To get there from Sisters, drive about 5.5 miles northwest on Highway 20/126 to the turnoff for Forest Road 11, which is paved but not necessarily well maintained. This is also known as the Indian Ford Junction. Turn here and drive almost 4 miles to the turnoff for Forest Road 1110. There's not much of a pullout space here, but do your best to park off the road, which does get some use during the winter.

Again, the preferred route here is to climb Forest Road 1110 until it ends, which is about a 3- to 4-mile investment. But you're not done there. The road ends at about 4,800 feet and you've still got another 2 miles to go on the trail to the summit. The road is straightforward and easy-going except for its steady uphill grade. The trail to the top turns into a stiffer climb, but before long you'll break out of the trees and walk above timberline on the upper cinder fields of Black Butte.

The other, more direct route, again, is to just head for the top regardless of trails. Only experienced snowshoers with a tolerance for serious bushwacking should consider this route. The forests look thin enough from the highway and even from the base of Forest Road 1110, but it's a false impression. Before long the well-spaced poles of ponderosa pine give way to a mixed conifer forest that confounds navigation and makes forward progress difficult. But you needn't worry about losing your way here. If you're bushwhacking, just push onward and upward, and don't bother trying to find alternative routes. You'll notice that just as you're about out of patience the forest does indeed clear out. Consider starting this sort of an ascent from Forest Road 1110 at the junction with summer hiking trails that go around the base of Black Butte.

--5*1*--
Tam McArthur Rim/Three Creek Lake

Rating:	More difficult
Round trip:	13 miles for Tam McArthur Rim; 10 miles for Three Creek Lake
Starting elevation:	5,120 feet
High point:	Tam McArthur Rim, 7,600 feet; Three Creek Lake, 6,560 feet
Best season:	December through April
Maps:	Geo-Graphics, Three Sisters Wilderness Map; USGS Broken Top
Who to contact:	Deschutes National Forest, Sisters Ranger District, (541) 549-7700

Try this route during the midweek, when you're less likely to run into snowmobiles. The road into Three Creek Lake is the quickest access to Tam

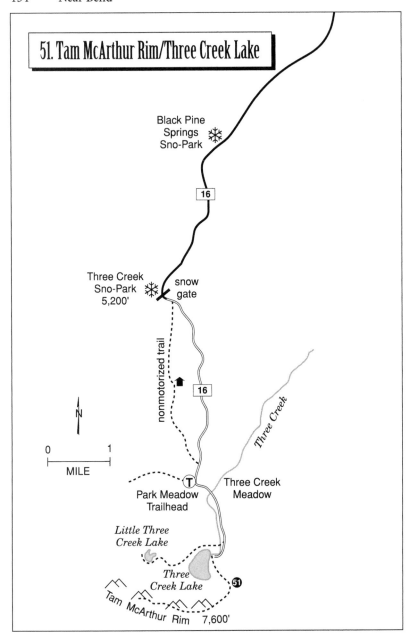

51. Tam McArthur Rim/Three Creek Lake

Black Pine
Springs
Sno-Park

16

Three Creek
Sno-Park
5,200'

snow
gate

nonmotorized trail

16

N

0   1
MILE

Three Creek

T

Park Meadow
Trailhead

Three Creek
Meadow

Little Three
Creek Lake

Three
Creek Lake

51

Tam McArthur Rim   7,600'

McArthur Rim, a dramatic formation that forms a natural coliseum around
the lake. The formation is named for Lewis A. "Tam" McArthur, a scholar

of Oregon's history and geography and the author of *Oregon Geographic Names*. Through his work with the Oregon Geographic Board, McArthur advised many of the early mapmakers and surveyors of Oregon. His invaluable reference book, which traces the genealogy of Oregon's diverse place names, has been updated and revised by his son, Lewis L. McArthur.

Those who venture to the top of the rim will get stunning views (on a clear day) of Mount Bachelor, the Three Sisters, Mount Jefferson, and possibly Mount Hood. Save your film, because you'll be tempted to spend it all on the magnificent panorama of Oregon's Cascades.

There are two ways to the lake. One way is to stay on the main road, which is direct but potentially monotonous and crowded with snowmobiles. The second way—a nicer, quieter route to the lake— is to take a separate trail for skiers and snowshoers that is closed off to snowmobiles. This side route adds a mile each way, but offers the benefit of peace and quiet. If you take this route remember to stay off the ski tracks.

To get there, drive first to Sisters, about 22 miles northwest of Bend on Highway 20. Once in Sisters, watch for Elm Street and turn south. Follow this road, which becomes Forest Road 16, until it ends at the snow level or a snow gate, whichever comes first. If the road is clear to the snow gate,

View of Mounts Jefferson and Hood from Tam McArthur Rim

you'll have gone about 11 miles. Park at the Three Creek Sno-Park, where you'll need to have a sno-park permit. The all-road version of this tour starts at the snow gate and climbs steadily uphill. Most of the route is uphill, but the road levels out a bit after a mile and a half. As you gain elevation, you can see the Three Sisters through the trees to the west.

At one-third mile, pass a junction with the nonmotorized route; the nonmotorized route reconnects with Forest Road 16 at approximately 3 miles. Up around the hill from this, get your first view of the rim. At a trail junction go left, following the combined blue and orange diamonds. At 4.5 miles, reach the Park Meadow Trailhead. Just around the bend from this, come to Three Creek Meadow with a dramatic view of Tam McArthur Rim beyond. Stay on the trail and cross Three Creek; begin to climb uphill toward the Three Creek Campground sign. A mile from here is Three Creek Lake, at the base of Tam McArthur Rim. As you near the lake, the vegetation changes; mountain hemlock trees will now be mixed in with lodgepole pines. The hemlocks are a sign of your advanced elevation; the lake stands at about 6,500 feet.

On a clear day, take advantage of the views on top of the rim. To get there, take the sloping ridge on the western edge of the rim. Follow this to several vantage points above 7,000 feet, which offer panoramic views of the Three Sisters and possibly Mount Hood.

--*52*--
Crater Lake Loop/Rim Drive

Rating: Most difficult/backcountry
Round trip: 33 miles
Starting elevation: 7,100 feet at Rim Village
High point: 7,700 feet
Best season: January through May
Maps: National Park Service, Crater Lake National Park; USFS Umpqua National Forest; USGS Crater Lake National Park
Who to contact: Crater Lake National Park, (541) 594-2211

This trip is one of Oregon's classics, the kind that's good to pull out of your braggart's hat at a cocktail party. It's a real commitment of time (allow 3 to 4 days), effort, and backcountry know-how. Crater Lake is as beautiful as it is bizarre; it was formed from the remnants of a massive volcano with wa-

Wizard Island in Crater Lake

ters so pure and still that on a windless winter day you might think you could walk across. It may be Oregon's only national park, but it's a doozy. Bring a camera loaded with film, because every new lake vista demands that you blow a few more frames.

It would be folly to think that, because you're following a road the entire duration of the trip, you're not going to need map, compass, or navigational skills. In fact, it's pretty darned easy to get lost out here because the road isn't always visible—and neither is the lake. Contrary to its name, Rim Road does not run along the absolute edge of Crater Lake. Instead, it winds back and forth, sometimes a long distance from the water. In white-out conditions there are plenty of places to get turned around, especially on the bluffs below Mount Scott.

Finally, there are a few avalanche-prone areas, primarily the steep slopes just below The Watchman, a landmark just west of Wizard Island, as well as the roadbed south of Applegate Peak and Sun Notch. The park service recommends that you wear an avalanche beacon, especially for these areas. The park rangers, who will sign you up for your backcountry users' permit (which is free), can brief you about the avalanche bypass routes so you can avoid these areas. Pencil the bypass routes into your map.

Crater Lake National Park is located in south-central Oregon, about 145 miles south of Bend and 175 miles southeast of Eugene. Its odd location usually lends itself to large amounts of snow accumulation, especially during late spring storms. During the winter only the south entrance is open, and the road is plowed only to the Rim Village, where you'll find a cafeteria, a gift shop, and a small kiosk where a park ranger is usually on hand to issue permits and answer questions. Sometimes even this entry road to the Rim Village isn't plowed, so call ahead of time with questions about roads and route conditions. Don't forget that you must check in when you finish the route.

The route is generally done in a clockwise direction, starting from the Rim Village. It's well worth parking your car down at the closed park headquarters, however, because Rim Drive drops you out down there and it's more than 600 feet below the Rim Village. The last thing you'll want to do after this trip is slog uphill to your car.

Skiers have done this route in a single day, but that's just not feasible for mere mortal snowshoers. Besides, doing this trip in a day means you're focusing on the next mile, not the stunning scenery or the peace of the backcountry. Plan your days accordingly. The first 6 miles to the North Junction feature the steep slopes of The Watchman, but are otherwise relatively open terrain with spotty forest. Several viewpoints along this first stretch offer enticing lake views.

In the section between the North Junction and the Cloudcap Over-

Camp at Crater Lake

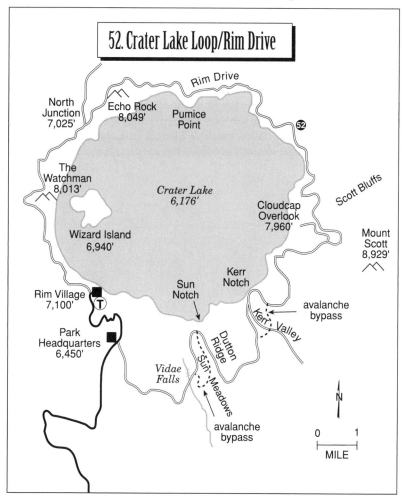

52. Crater Lake Loop/Rim Drive

Rim Drive

North Junction
7,025'

Echo Rock
8,049'

Pumice
Point

52

The Watchman
8,013'

Crater Lake
6,176'

Scott Bluffs

Cloudcap
Overlook
7,960'

Wizard Island
6,940'

Mount
Scott
8,929'

Kerr
Notch

Sun
Notch

Rim Village
7,100'

T

avalanche
bypass

Kerr Valley

Park
Headquarters
6,450'

Dutton Ridge

Vidae
Falls

Sun Meadows

N

avalanche
bypass

0   1
MILE

look area, another 11 miles, the terrain can be difficult to navigate. As you approach Mount Scott and the bluffs below that mountain, keep your eyes on your compass, especially in poor weather. As the terrain flattens out, it's harder to tell where the road goes. Some 'shoers mistake the road to the Cloudcap Overlook for Rim Drive.

On the southeastern portion of the route, the road starts winding in and out of drainages and notches in the crater rim. Two of these are the most prominent: Kerr Notch, which is at mile 21, and Sun Notch, at mile 25. Kerr Notch is the first area along the route to have a fully signed avalanche bypass. This bypass trail runs through the steep forests and keeps you from going under the cliffs of Dutton Ridge, so you don't need to worry about avalanche hazard. You'll add about 3 miles to the trip, but it's much safer.

Another avalanche bypass route just past Sun Notch climbs up out of Sun Meadows and back up to the road near Vidae Falls. From here the trail rolls gently up and down hill toward the park headquarters. You know you're getting close to the end when you see more and more skier and snowshoer tracks. Sun Notch is a popular day trip. Be sure to check back in with the rangers at headquarters before you leave the park.

View of Mount Bailey from across Diamond Lake

PART 4

Southern Oregon

--53--
Lake of the Woods/High Lakes Trail

Rating: More difficult
Round trip: 9 miles one way
Starting elevation: 4,600 feet
High point: 5,220 feet
Best season: January through March
Maps: USFS Sky Lakes Wilderness; USGS Mount McLoughlin
Who to contact: Rogue River National Forest, Ashland Ranger District, (541) 482-3333

In the summertime hikers and mountain bikers flock to this popular trail than runs through meadows of wildflowers. In the wintertime the scene changes dramatically; a hiker's eyes are lifted from the meadows and up into the surrounding mountains. Mount McLoughlin dominates the northern skyline, while 7,300-foot Brown Mountain is on the south. Nearby Fish Lake has a resort and is well known in southern Oregon for, well, fishing. In the winter things quiet down dramatically, and snowshoers will have only snowmobilers to relate to while they're here.

Along the way you'll be in the midst of the Brown Mountain lava flows, which you hope are well covered with snow. On a small portion of this hike you'll pass through an ancient southern Oregon conifer forest, but for most of the route you'll be awed by extensive views north and south. And if you start from the Fish Lake area, you'll intersect the Pacific Crest National Scenic Trail in the early portion of this hike.

Finally, there's only a slight, gradual elevation gain to consider. But because in the winter you can't count on extensive, visible trail markers, this route stays out of the "easy" category. You'll need a map and compass to make sure you're on track. Don't count on following another traveler's tracks out here.

This is a one-way trail best done with a shuttle at the Fish Lake Sno-Park and another at the Great Meadow Sno-Park. That way you don't have to backtrack and turn a manageable 9-mile hike into an 18-mile death march.

To start, drive 37 miles east from Medford on Highway 140. Keep an eye peeled for the Fish Lake Sno-Park, nestled near the shores of the lake. The Fish Lake Trail starts out as a shared route with snowmobilers. Enter a network of short cross-country ski trails here, and for the first segment follow signs for Lollipop Loop for about a half mile. Keep your eyes peeled for the Fish Lake tie-in trail and follow that for 1.5 miles to the Pacific Crest Trail junction. If you feel fatigued at this point, consider your escape possibilities; you could take the Pacific Crest Trail north and up to Highway 140, or loop back to the Fish Lake Sno-Park. After this junction, however, you are more or less committed to the High Lakes Trail.

In 6 miles come to the summertime trail to the top of Brown Mountain. Cross Forest Road 3640, where you could also bail out of the route if you needed to. But at this point, you're about 1.5 miles from the Great Meadow Sno-Park.

The terrain is fairly moderate here as you approach Lake of the Woods and the Great Meadow Sno-Park. Walk past the northern terminus of the lake, another summer trailhead, and another forest road before you finish out at the Great Meadow Sno-Park, where your shuttle is waiting. Don't forget the keys.

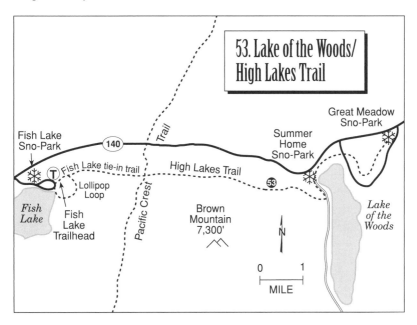

--*54*--
Pelican Butte

Rating: Most difficult
Round trip: 9 miles
Starting elevation: 5,800 feet
High point: 8,036 feet
Best season: April through June
Maps: USFS Sky Lakes Wilderness
Who to contact: Winema National Forest, Klamath Ranger District, (541) 885-3400

Consider this an "endangered trail," because if the political winds shift, this area might become a ski resort. Developers in Klamath Falls are itching to turn Pelican Butte into a year-round resort area, forever changing the nature of this stellar wildlife viewing spot. But while it's intact, Pelican Butte is a marvelous landmark in the Klamath Basin area. The spot is a well-known haunt for bald eagles and other wilderness creatures. It's no wonder that it has been nominated for wilderness area status to protect it from development and logging.

In the meantime, Pelican Butte offers great views of the Klamath Wildlife Refuge, Mount McLoughlin, and the Sky Lakes Wilderness Area. Sprawling old ponderosa pines, some hundreds of years old, cover the slopes of Pelican Butte. It's in these big old trees that you're most likely to glimpse bald eagles, which use their branches to spot their prey. Although Pelican Butte is named for the white pelicans that frequent the wildlife refuge, don't count on seeing any while you're on snowshoes. In the winter, they're far away in warmer climes. Instead watch for osprey, which fly up and down the wide basin.

Although you'll travel on a road the whole way, getting to the top of Pelican Butte is a serious endeavor. You'll trek 4.5 miles along the winding Forest Road 980 one way. The road climbs 2,000 feet before topping out at the summit of Pelican Butte and the site of an old lookout point.

To get to the base of Pelican Butte, drive east on Highway 140 from Medford toward Rocky Point, 40 to 45 miles. Approximately 4 miles before you get to Rocky Point, a turnoff that is well signed for Cold Springs in on the north side of the highway. Turn here and follow Forest Road 3651, which you hope is clear of snow for as much of its 11-mile distance as possible. It's a snowmobile route otherwise, and that's why you might want

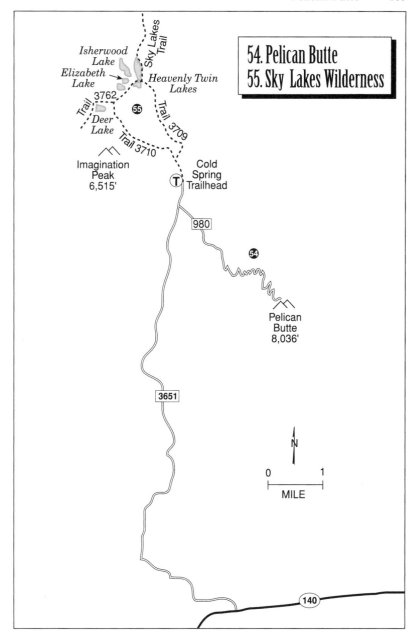

54. Pelican Butte
55. Sky Lakes Wilderness

Isherwood Lake
Elizabeth Lake
Sky Lakes Trail
Heavenly Twin Lakes
3762
55
Trail
Deer Lake
Trail 3709
Trail 3710
Imagination Peak
6,515'
Cold Spring Trailhead
T
980
54
Pelican Butte
8,036'
3651
N
0   1
MILE
140

to wait until the late spring to do this snowshoe route. Nothing like snowshoeing in shorts! The junction with Road 980 is just a couple of miles south from the Cold Springs Trailhead. Park at the junction and follow Road 980 uphill and to the west toward Pelican Butte.

For the first couple of miles, the road is fairly straight as it climbs toward the steeper portions of the butte. But at about 6,600 feet the switchbacks start in earnest and you'll begin to really pack in the elevation gain. This is still another reason to wait until late spring to do this route; by the time you get to a climb like this, you might have a winter's full of snowshoeing under your belt and such a climb won't lay waste to your quadriceps too early.

Pelican Butte was once a cinder cone, and the terrain begins to reflect this as you near the summit. The tree cover begins to get sparse, and you might see exposed boulders as you approach the top.

Bring a camera, because the view from atop Pelican Butte is stellar on a clear day.

-- 55 --
Sky Lakes Wilderness

Rating: More difficult
Round trip: 4 miles to Heavenly Twin Lakes
Starting elevation: 5,900 feet
High point: 6,200 feet
Best season: April through May
Maps: USFS Sky Lakes Wilderness
Who to contact: Winema National Forest, Klamath Ranger District, (541) 885-3400

This is a perfectly manageable march into the southern Oregon woods, and what you get after only 2 miles of hiking is a group of truly beautiful wilderness lakes. The Sky Lakes Wilderness is peppered with these hidden water holes, and in the winter they become even more beguiling. After passing a few frozen-over ponds, puddles, and potholes, you'll first reach the Heavenly Twin Lakes. Plan to make the Heavenly Twins your day's destination (even if there's little about them to suggest a twin existence). It's clear that they are indeed heavenly, but then what lake in the woods is not?

The best access to this route is via the Cold Spring Trailhead. To get to Cold Spring Trailhead, drive east on Highway 140 from Medford toward Rocky Point, a distance of about 40 to 45 miles. About 4 miles before you get to Rocky Point, a turnoff that is well signed for Cold Springs is on the north side of the highway. Turn here and pick up Forest Road 3651, an unpaved forest road that takes you to the trailhead in 11 miles. If Forest Road 3651 is closed, you must find another trailhead

The Cold Springs Trailhead might still be snowed-in if the winter has been heavy enough. When there's snow here, the Forest Service closes off this road and leaves it to the snowmobilers, making late spring/early summer the best time for snowshoers to come. Until the gate is lifted, it's reserved entirely for their use. Although there's nothing really stopping you from snowshoeing up the road, be aware that you're not the primary user here.

At the Cold Spring Trailhead there are some dilapidated shelters and a camping area. Head north on the trail here and immediately enter the shaggy woods.

The trail doesn't gain much in the way of elevation here, wandering gently uphill. In about a half mile, reach a junction where you can go straight (left) and take the Cold Spring Trail 3710 into the lake basin. My preference, though, is to take a right here and follow the South Rock Creek Trail 3709 to the lakes. This trail follows the rim of a canyon into the wilderness and offers better views down toward the Klamath Marsh and, to the southeast, Pelican Butte. Here you travel above the headwaters of Rock Creek and look down into its substantial canyon. The mix of pine and fir trees creates a lot of forest openings and sun breaks along the trail. As you get closer to the lakes, however, notice that you will once again enter the deeper forest. Here there are amazing stands of old-growth forest punctuated by small puddles and potholes—previews of the lakes to come.

There are almost too many lakes here to tell which is which. When you get to the junction with the Sky Lakes Trail, you're on the doorstep of the Sky Lakes Basin, and it's hard to walk more than a mile in this area without coming across another lake. The Heavenly Twin Lakes start on your left or just to the south of the trail; the partner is right across the trail. But don't just stop there; wander around to Isherwood Lake, also nearby, and Elizabeth Lake, Lake Notasha, and little Lake Liza, also in the neighborhood.

It's easy to get lost traipsing around between all these lakes, and you shouldn't try to cross these lakes even though they might look frozen solid. They change depths dramatically from one end to another, and you could easily walk off one section of hard-frozen lake water and into another, less consolidated spot.

From here you can either go back the way you came and catch the views of Pelican Butte as you go, or make the loop down the Cold Spring Trail 3710 back to the trailhead. If you do that, make sure to stay to the left at the junction with Trail 3762 toward Deer Lake. You pass beneath 6,515-foot

Imagination Peak if you take this route, so be aware of terrain traps or possible avalanche hazard during a heavy winter.

--*56*--
Cherry Creek to Sky Lakes

Rating: More difficult
Round trip: 10 miles
Starting elevation: 4,500 feet
High point: 6,000 feet
Best season: January through April
Maps: USFS Sky Lakes Wilderness
Who to contact: Winema National Forest, Klamath Ranger District, (541) 885-3400

Here's another southern Oregon ancient forest ramble that shows off the area's diversity of tree species. In any given mile of this tough route you'll be wandering through stands of massive old white fir, ponderosa pine, or Englemann spruce. If you stick it out for the last grueling mile or two, you'll be rewarded by your arrival at Trapper Lake and the beautiful Sky Lakes Basin.

A word of caution: Cherry Creek potentially could be a "terrain trap" for avalanches because it sits at the bottom of a deep valley between the impressive Cherry Peak (6,623 feet) and Lather Mountain (6,945 feet). That means while there's no possibility of your riding an avalanche down a hill, you could be hiking at the bottom of several avalanche paths. When you plan your trip, check in with local resources and weather reports, or wait until later in the spring when the snowpack is more stable.

To get to Cherry Creek, take Highway 140 east from Medford toward Rocky Point, about 45 miles. Take County Road 531, West Side Road, about 6.5 miles north along the edge of the Klamath Marsh. On the west side of the road, turn left onto Forest Road 3450, which is signed for the Cherry Creek Trail. Drive as far up this unpaved road as you can; the trailhead is in 2 miles.

The trail drops down into the creek bottom and begins winding almost due west from the trailhead. Walk about a half mile, then enter the Sky Lakes Wilderness. For the first several miles there is little to no elevation gain, making for a pleasant snowshoe outing when the conditions are right. The valley bottom you're walking in is punctuated by beautiful groves

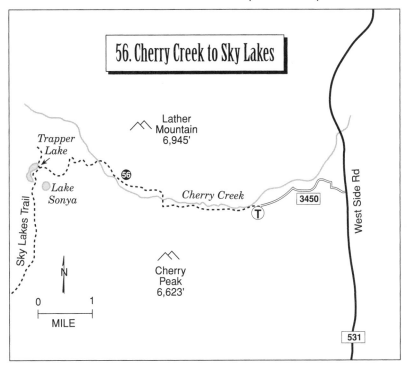

56. Cherry Creek to Sky Lakes

Lather Mountain 6,945'

Trapper Lake

Lake Sonya

Cherry Creek

56

3450

West Side Rd

Sky Lakes Trail

N

Cherry Peak 6,623'

0 1

MILE

531

of older spruce trees. Keep a heads-up when you're on this route, because you're not only surrounded by very large trees, but you're also in the midst of a lot of different bird life, including bald eagles. This is the edge of two ecosystems: the forests of the Sky Lakes Wilderness and the marsh of the Klamath Basin. There are also occasional breaks in the thick forest canopy that might allow for views of the two peaks that flank this canyon, especially Cherry Peak.

After about 3.5 miles, come to the head of the Cherry Creek canyon, where the summer trail begins to climb steeply toward the lake basin. Walk just north of a Cherry Creek tributary and again hike due west with occasional switchbacks to the summit of the ridge. Trapper Lake is the first large lake that comes into view. Lake Sonya is off to the south of the trail.

This route is designed to end at Trapper Lake, right about where the Cherry Creek Trail connects with Trail 3739 that travels north and south through the Sky Lakes Basin. From here you're about a mile from the junction with the Pacific Crest National Scenic Trail. There really aren't any loop options available to take you back to the trailhead here, but you could make the trip quite a bit longer by looping around the Sky Lakes Basin. If you do so, monitor the daylight and your own fatigue.

--57--
Diamond Lake

Rating: More difficult
Round trip: 4 miles
Starting elevation: 5,400 feet
High point: 6,300 feet
Best season: January through March
Maps: USFS Umpqua National Forest; USGS Mount Thielsen
Who to contact: Umpqua National Forest, Diamond Lake Ranger District, (541) 498-2531

Diamond Lake is a massive landmark in south-central Oregon. The large number of trails available make it practically a destination snowshoeing center if you have time for more than just one route. A good representative trail is the 4-mile Silent Creek Loop, located among the Silent Creek trails on the southwest side of Diamond Lake. Besides snowshoeing, the Diamond Lake area has something for everyone.

The Diamond Lake Resort, a cross-country ski resort, offers overnight lodging and other facilities. The 8,363-foot Mount Bailey, located off the western shores of the lake, is the focus for a snow-cat ski guide service that is famous for steep powder skiing. Diamond Lake itself is huge, 2 miles by 3 miles wide. From its shores you'll have astounding views of Mount Bailey's substantial girth to the towering spire of Mount Thielsen. It's also a seasonal host to bald eagles passing through on a winter migratory pattern. If you come here later in the winter and spring you're likely to spot one of these majestic birds from the lakeshore.

To get to the Diamond Lake area, take Highway 97 to the turnoff for Highway 138, east of Crater Lake National Park. Drive west on Highway 138 for about 16 miles, and then turn west onto Highway 230, the West Diamond Highway, which heads toward Medford. The Three Lakes Sno-Park is just 3 miles from Highway 138 on Highway 230.

From the Three Lakes Sno-Park walk up Forest Road 3703, which is a

Snowshoe tracks

popular snowmobiler's route up toward Mount Bailey. Fortunately you stay on the road for only about 100 yards or so before turning right into the woods on the Silent Creek Trail. Cross Silent Creek itself within a mile, and at approximately the 1.5-mile point, cross the trail that climbs up to Hemlock Butte and, beyond that, Mount Bailey. If you go straight, or right, here, you'll eventually reach the lakeshore, which offers good views.

To return, you can either go back the way you came or make a longer loop by going over 6,300-foot Hemlock Butte. This area is dominated by lodgepole pine trees, which offer a lot of sunlight breaks. In just under 3 miles from the junction of the Silent Creek and Mount Bailey Trails, come to a classic A-frame cabin, which the forest service rents out through a reservation system. In a few hundred yards come to an old forest road, No. 380. Take a left here and drop down toward the main Mount Bailey Road in another 1.5 miles. It's just 2 miles from this junction back to the east and the Three Lakes Sno-Park.

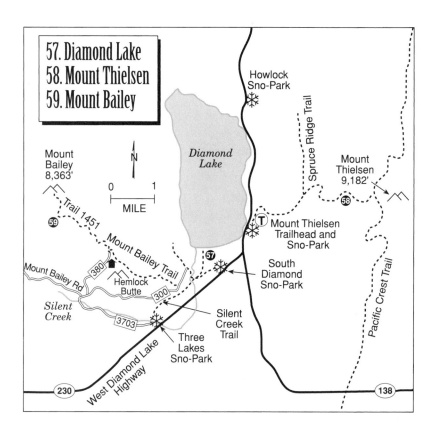

--58--
Mount Thielsen

Rating: Most difficult/backcountry
Round trip: 10 miles
Starting elevation: 5,200 feet
High point: 8,000 feet
Best season: January through June
Maps: USGS Mount Thielsen; USFS Mount Thielsen Wilderness
Who to contact: Umpqua National Forest, Diamond Lake Ranger District, (541) 498-2531

Few of Oregon's signature Cascades has as dramatic a profile as Mount Thielsen. It's one of the state's most overlooked peaks, perhaps only because it's not located conveniently at the edge of a major metropolitan area. None of the other Cascades juts as pointedly into the skyline as this peak does. It has inspired mountaineers for decades, if only after they've had their fill of Mount Hood's crowded slopes.

This route does not detail the full climb to the top of Mount Thielsen, because getting there in the winter (snowshoeing season) involves serious mountaineering skills. Instead, the route leads to a beautiful ridge that takes you right to the base of the summit spire, with expansive views of the Diamond Lake and Crater Lake country. From this spot, even Mount Bailey looks like a low hump on the horizon. Also, you can do this route as late as June or even July, depending on the snow year. You might have some dirty snow at the forested base, but in general this is a great hill to head for when the sun is shining and the days are longer. Located as it is in the southwestern Oregon mountains near Crater Lake, its weather is generally more favorable than the west side of the Cascades; there is more sun here and less prevailing fog and mist.

This route is intended for the snowshoer with a good bit of stamina and superb navigational skills; the trail here isn't as well marked as it could be and there are plenty of confusing spots.

To get to the trailhead, drive on Highway 138 west from Highway 97 to the Thielsen Sno-Park. The sno-park is just 2.7 miles south of Howlock Sno-Park and barely 1.5 miles north of the junction with Highway 230. The trail from the Thielson Sno-Park is marked with blue diamonds, but because the route takes some confusing twists and turns, watch closely for the next blue diamond and follow your progress on your map. At 1.5 miles, pass the junction with the Spruce Ridge Trail. Go straight here and continue to contour up the hill for another half mile, after which you'll cross into the Mount Thielsen Wilderness Area. The forest here is mostly lodgepole pine with some larger Englemann spruce and subalpine fir species. Note that the blue diamond markers disappear once you cross the wilderness boundary. Soon after passing into the wilderness, however, you'll get an excellent view of Thielsen that should put your direction into perspective.

Now aim east toward the Pacific Crest National Scenic Trail, which passes at the 7,000-foot level below the base of Mount Thielsen. At the intersection with the Pacific Crest Trail (7,320 feet), gaze upon the stunning viewpoint here of the mountain looming overhead.

You could stop here, set up a lunch spot, and call it good for the day—or you could climb a little bit higher.

Mount Thielsen

--*59*--
Mount Bailey

Rating:	Most difficult
Round trip:	9 miles
Starting elevation:	5,800 feet from Forest Road 300
High point:	8,363 feet
Best season:	March through May
Maps:	USFS Umpqua National Forest
Who to contact:	Umpqua National Forest, Diamond Lake Ranger District, (541) 498-2531

Mount Bailey offers a great contrast to Mount Thielsen across the way. Its rounded mellow slopes make for a lot of walking for the elevation gain, while Thielsen demands the hiker to make a lot of altitude in a hurry. For the most part this is a great straightforward march up a beautiful old volcano that gets you up above Diamond Lake and gives you a view across the way to Mount Thielsen. This is a perfect climb for someone who's in great shape but not necessarily technically oriented. There just aren't too many challenges on the way to the summit other than navigational issues. Keep in mind, however, as you merrily march up the hill that this is an avalanche-prone area.

The mountain is also the prime territory for a snow-cat skiing operation. Although you can see the snow cats on the hill, whether they're driving up or skiing down, don't count on them to keep track of you; the guides have their hands full with their clients.

Why the late season for Bailey? When you wait until the snow melts off of the lower roads, you can drive in a lot closer to this mountain—and there will still be plenty of snow where you'll be hiking. If you start the route from the Three Lakes Sno-Park, you will add 4 round-trip miles onto the hike. From the Three Lakes Sno-Park, follow Forest Road 3703 for 2 miles and 600 feet of elevation gain to the junction with Forest Road 300, which isn't well marked. (This area is also popular with snowmobilers, making a midweek trip a little more appealing.)

To get there drive west from Highway 97 to the turnoff for Highway 138 toward Diamond Lake. After about 16 miles on Highway 138 turn west onto Highway 230, the West Diamond Lake Highway. The Three Lakes Sno-Park is 3 miles down that road toward Medford. You should hope at this point that the snow is off Forest Road 3703 and that you can drive to

Mount Bailey, behind Diamond Lake

the junction with Road 300, about 2 miles away. At the junction with Road 300, which is a very primitive road, hike to the turnoff for Hemlock Butte, which follows primitive Road 380. This road pushes into a wide steep basin, which puts you in a bit of avalanche terrain.

The Hemlock Butte Trail climbs to about 6,300 feet before it junctions with Trail 1451, which leads to the summit of Mount Bailey. Keep in mind that few of the markers or the trails may be visible during a heavy snow year. From this point, climb on about 2,000 vertical feet and 3 miles to the summit. Walk right between two steep bowls on the north and south of you. The ridge gets progressively steeper and narrower near the summit.

At about 7,700 feet walk very carefully around a rocky old crater that sits below an aggravating false summit. Take a deep breath and step carefully up here; it's likely to be pretty hairy. The snow quality can be poor from the sun and wind rotting, and the steep slopes may seem to fall away from you. The final push to the summit is nothing short of intimidating as you ridge-walk all the way. In fact, bring hiking poles for this part of the route; you'll be glad for the stability they offer.

--60--
Mount McLoughlin

Rating: Most difficult
Round trip: 10 miles
Starting elevation: 5,500 feet
High point: 9,495 feet
Best season: February through May
Maps: USFS Sky Lakes Wilderness
Who to contact: Winema National Forest, Klamath Ranger District, (541) 885-3400

Mount McLoughlin dominates the views around the Klamath Basin and Lake of the Woods area and makes a worthy goal for any intrepid snowshoer. There's nothing like looking down on the massive lakes far below. On a clear day the views stretch deep into northern California, where Mount

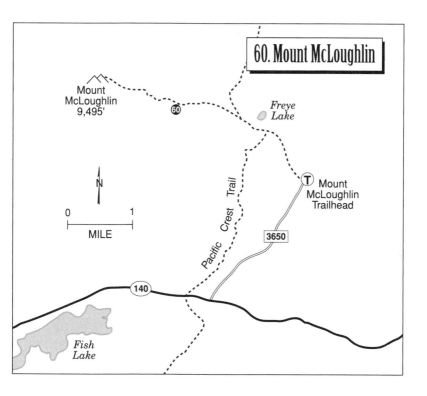

Shasta appears as a small white triangle in the distance. To the north you can see the rim of Crater Lake. At well over 9,000 feet, this is the tallest landmark for miles and certainly the highest point in the Sky Lakes Wilderness. It was formed by volcanic action and has assumed an almost perfectly conical shape, which makes it pretty simple to navigate.

As mountains go, this is a relatively straightforward climb, even though it has all the expected alpine hazards, such as avalanche potential and bad weather. That's why you should time this climb for late winter or early spring. Again, you're guaranteed longer days and more stable weather during March and April. May is pushing it for this hike, but if it has been a heavy snow year, you can practically do the route in shirtsleeves—just be prepared for foul weather if it arises.

Looking down upon Mount McLoughlin with a map or from an airplane, you might not think much of a climb up this mountain. As the crow flies, this is a short trip. But you'll actually climb hundreds of feet per mile on the 5-mile hike to the summit. Come prepared with hiking poles, a map, a compass, and even an altimeter to keep on track. Even if you haven't used them before, bring hiking poles for the steep angle of ascent and descent. If the snow is soft, as is likely in a spring ascent, the poles come in handy for hauling yourself out of postholes. Also, keep in mind that there isn't a marked trail. You'll follow a prominent ridge up the mountain, and in years gone by some climbers have left flagging or other markers, but since this is a wilderness area you shouldn't count on any such man-made garbage to guide your way.

Start by driving east from Medford on Highway 140 for about 30 miles.

Mount McLoughlin

Turn north onto Forest Road 3650, which is just over a mile past the Fish Lake Campground, and is signed for the Summit Trail, or Mount McLoughlin Trailhead. The trailhead gets frequent use and will be obvious. Which brings me to another point: this area is popular with backcountry skiers and snowboarders who make the long drive down from Bend or the Willamette Valley. If you're sharing the mountain with them, don't blindly follow their tracks—they might choose different routes up, and certainly down, the mountain.

From the trailhead, hike in about 1.5 miles to the junction with the Pacific Crest National Scenic Trail. You might also see a small trail headed off to Freye Lake. Stay with the trail heading west; when you reach the second junction with the Pacific Crest Trail, keep left (straight). During heavy snow, none of the trails will necessarily be visible, so navigating in these woods may be difficult.

Notice now that tree line is coming up, and the trail is getting steeper. Crest a ridge that you shouldn't by any means mistake for the summit. Once you break free of the timber, you should see the long eastern ridge of the mountain; follow this landmark directly to the top. If you can't see the ridgeline that means the weather is lousy and you ought to consider an early turnaround time. Because McLoughlin is so conical in shape you can wander off route pretty easily in a snowstorm.

Once you get onto the ridge and get up above the trees, you'll see that the northern side of the ridge, to your right, drops off somewhat precipitously. By the time the terrain looks like this, you've got about 1,500 feet to go to the summit.

Snowshoeing in the Wallowa Mountains

PART 5

Eastern Oregon

--61--
Aneroid Lake

Rating: Most difficult
Round trip: 12 miles
Starting elevation: 4,645 feet
High point: 7,500 feet
Best season: December through March
Maps: Imus Geographics, Wallowa Mountains; USGS Aneroid Mountain
Who to contact: Wallowa–Whitman National Forest, Wallowa Valley Ranger District, (541) 426-4978

Aneroid Lake shines like a gem in the midst of Wallowa Mountain splendor. Surrounded by rugged ridges, the lake gives you the feeling you're in some godly amphitheater. All around you are the lesser Wallowa peaks such

Aneroid Peak

as Jewett and Petes Point. The gradual route into the lake basin allows you to gain the necessary elevation by increments instead of a grueling push. Enjoy the views along the way, including the canyon of the East Fork Wallowa River and the rugged and rocky cliffs above the trail.

Plan to camp by the shores of Aneroid Lake, which is well frozen but still unsafe for walking. Otherwise it's a long haul back down to the trailhead. You may be tempted to investigate some cabins tucked into the woods to the southeast of the lake. These cabins are privately owned, however, and not intended for public use. Please respect the privacy of the owners and steer clear of these.

Also, as you prepare for the trip, keep in mind that the weather pattern in the Wallowas can be less predictable than in other parts of the state. Even late in March major snowstorms can whip up and bury the mountains in several inches of new snow. This can be titillating or frustrating, depending on your attitude. The Wallowa Lake Trailhead is just past the southern end of Wallowa Lake, a major scenic attraction in and of itself. From the town of Joseph, drive south 6 miles on Highway 82 and around the eastern shore of Wallowa Lake. This is a good time to look high into the mountains to the south and see just what sort of weather inhabits the upper valleys. Skip the turnoff for Wallowa Lake State Park and turn toward the campground and powerhouse at the end of the road. There's a paved parking area and a stock loading bay right in front of the trailhead.

At 4,645 feet the trailhead is seldom very snowy. You'll probably start this hike in just your boots, with your snowshoes in hand or on your backpack. Take the East Fork of the Wallowa River Trail, No. 1804, and start up a series of switchbacks that quickly begin climbing out of the valley. It takes about 1 to 1.5 miles to get past the drone of the powerhouse, but before long the forests swallow you up and the only white noise you will hear is the rushing of the river.

At the 1.5-mile mark come right to the edge of the river and see a bridge across it. This is the way back down the hill on an old road that isn't worth taking up or down. Instead stay on the trail as it turns up and away from the river here and begins gaining elevation in a more orderly fashion.

Watch out for a few dicey spots along the way, including some steep, open slopes created by avalanches. Also, if you suddenly walk out of the woods and onto a steep slope without any tall trees on it, you're in the path of avalanches. Some of these slopes are quite steep; cross them carefully.

Several miles up the trail, come to a wooden footbridge (probably covered in snow) that crosses the river in a dense lodgepole pine forest. The trail levels out considerably here, but the routefinding becomes trickier. As

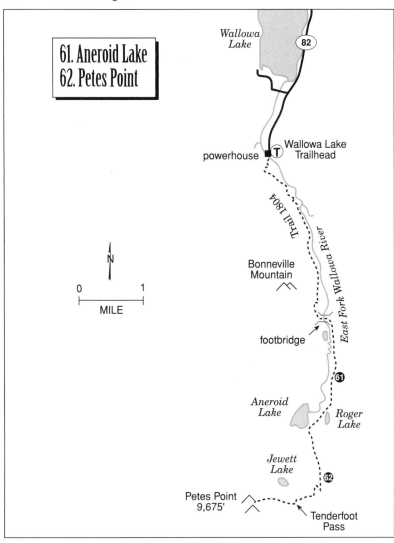

the terrain flattens out, it's harder to track the path of the river, so keep your map and compass handy. You can tell you're nearing Aneroid Lake when you see the much smaller Roger Lake to the southeast of Aneroid and when you notice the topography change. Aneroid is virtually at the end of what could be described as a massive box canyon; you can see the ridgeline on the west start to turn and wrap around the end of the lake basin. Find good campsites on the north end of the lake.

--62--
Petes Point

Rating: Backcountry
Round trip: 7 miles from Aneroid Lake
Starting elevation: 7,500 feet at Aneroid Lake
High point: 9,675 feet
Best season: February through May
Maps: Imus Geographics, Wallowa Mountains; USGS Aneroid Mountain
Who to contact: Wallowa–Whitman National Forest, Wallowa Mountains Visitors Center, (541) 426-5546

Got an extra day while camping at Aneroid Lake? Here's a chance to get above it all in the Wallowas and really see the mountain range the way it should be seen. Petes Point juts up above the Aneroid Lake basin with views that show you just how vast and rugged this mountain range is. From the top of Petes Point, you can see in all directions, from the spreading plains, to the north of the Wallowas, to the jagged jumble of peaks on all other sides.

Petes Point makes for a good challenge for experienced backcountry snowshoers. Stay on alert at all times for hazardous cornices and avalanche conditions. And be prepared to wear your boots—not your snowshoes—for at least part of the time. Some portions of the upper peak are such a thin ridgeline that you might want to cautiously do the postholing necessary to cross the hazardous upper ridges. Hiking poles come in handy for safety and fatigue. Also, everyone in your group should wear an avalanche beacon and carry a shovel, should they need to dig someone out of a slide.

The trailhead is located just past the southern end of Wallowa Lake. From the town of Joseph, drive 6 miles south on Highway 82 and around the eastern shore of Wallowa Lake. Skip the turnoff for Wallowa Lake State Park and turn toward the campground and powerhouse at the end of the road. There's a paved parking area and a stock loading bay right in front of the trailhead.

Follow the directions in Route 61 to Aneroid Lake. From Aneroid Lake continue south past the private cabins and up the drainage that feeds into the lake. Hike through this canyon for about 2 miles before you climb out onto Tenderfoot Pass. Along the way, glimpse Aneroid Mountain, an almost

Petes Point

perfect cone of a peak. That's another good destination, but also fraught with avalanche hazard and not necessarily as easy to access as Petes Point.

Below and to the west is a small basin for Jewett Lake. In fact, the canyon that falls away to the north of this lake leads directly back to Aneroid, but because of its steep walls I don't recommend using it as a return route.

Instead, turn your gaze up to Petes Point, looming above Jewett Lake. The prominent east-west ridge that descends to a wide apron in front of you is the route to take to the summit. If avalanche hazard is low, it's easier to walk around the south side of the ridge and climb up the side. The lower ridge portions are craggy and precipitous.

At this point notice that Petes Point has a concave aspect on its east side, where the summit ridge wraps around in a ∪ shape. Don't get too deep into this terrain feature. You're already in prime avalanche terrain by climbing up onto the ridge of Petes. Don't push your luck.

This summit ridge of Petes Point is awfully narrow at certain points, and the mountainsides drop away steeply in either direction. Be aware that this mountain develops heavy cornices after storms and high winds, so make sure that you're not putting your weight or stress onto a chunk of snow that's barely holding on. Be smart up here and evaluate your route as you go. Don't try this route in inclement weather, since it's easy to lose your way up on the summit ridge.

Once you near the top, several false summits will present themselves. If you push due west you'll get to the top of the northern summit. The true summit, at 9,675 feet, is around the ∪ shape of the ridge and to the south.

There's also a good chance that you'll see signs of mountain goats here. From time to time the elusive creatures wander up onto Petes Point in the early spring, leaving their dainty tracks in the most precarious of spots. Don't try to follow them around this mountain; they've been doing it for much longer than you have. Keep your camera handy in case you might actually see them, although their white coats make them difficult to spot.

--63--
Wagon Road Trail

Rating: More difficult
Round trip: 8 miles
Starting elevation: 6,100 feet
High point: 6,400 feet
Best season: January through March
Maps: Imus Geographics, Wallowa Mountains
Who to contact: Wallowa–Whitman National Forest, Wallowa Mountains Visitors Center, (541) 426-5546

The Seven Devils Mountains don't look as if they belong in the Pacific Northwest, where we are accustomed to massive volcanoes standing alone in the landscape. These Idaho peaks are almost otherworldly looking in the way they claw at the sky, and this route will show you why. Similarly, the Wallowa Mountains, which this route pokes into, often have been called by the comical nickname "America's Little Switzerland," because of their rugged jumble of peaks and valleys, standing in dramatic contrast to the peak-and-plain geography of western Oregon. This route not only will whet your appetite for more Wallowas exploration, but also will show you that it takes a bit of work to get into them. Much of the trail here passes through the site of the Canal fire of 1989, so expect a lot of openings with dramatic vistas to the east.

The Wagon Road Trail follows a generally southward route toward the Big Sheep Cutoff Trail, a half-mile trail that drops down a steep hill. Don't bother with that trail at the end; it's used mostly by backcountry skiers headed deeper into the backcountry. In fact this route is used by

Wing Ridge Ski Tours to access a shelter system in the Big Sheep drainage. Be aware of trail etiquette here and be sure to use different parts of the trail than the skiers.

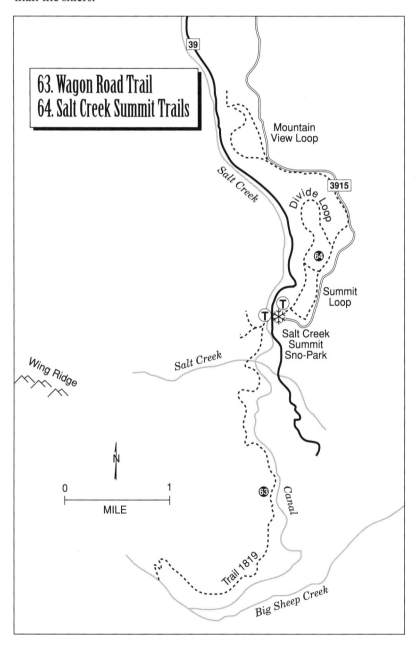

Frozen tree in the Wallowa Mountains

Start at the Salt Creek Summit Sno-Park, 12 miles south of the town of Joseph on Forest Road 39, also called the Hells Canyon Scenic Byway. To get there, drive out of Joseph on the Imnaha Highway 350 and turn right on Forest Road 39. The sno-park is a little more than 7 miles up the road. From the sno-park walk back across the road and cross Salt Creek itself on a small bridge. Careful here: this bridge area gets congested. Several trails spill out right by the bridge, and most of them are on a descent path before they get there, meaning you should be nimble in case flying out-of-control skiers come your way.

Immediately across the bridge turn left and south onto Trail 1819; pass a junction with the Devils View Loop along the way. You'll walk above a canal for much of the trip, passing through various mixtures of burned and unburned forests and open meadows. Keep your eyes peeled here for the Seven Devils Mountains, way out to the east.

On your way south, encounter only a few mellow hills. The hill you're walking along is the base of Wing Ridge, a substantial landmark that forms first as a wide "wing" off of Aneroid Mountain above Aneroid Lake (Route 61). Fortunately this route more or less stays on a level contour as it rounds Wing Ridge.

After a while you will begin to see down into the Big Sheep Creek. As you near the creek the slope gets steeper, so be aware of potential avalanche hazard in this area. After about 4 miles come to the Big Sheep Cutoff Trail, which drops into the creek basin and accesses the ski shelters. This is effectively where this route ends; the trail back to the north and to the sno-park affords a casual descent back into the Salt Creek Summit area.

--64--
Salt Creek Summit Trails

Rating: Easy to moderate
Round trip: 1.3 miles for Summit Loop, 2.9 miles for Mountain View Loop
Starting elevation: 6,100 feet
High point: 6,200 feet for Summit Loop, 5,800 feet for Mountain View Loop
Best season: January through March
Maps: Imus Geographics, Wallowa Mountains
Who to contact: Wallowa–Whitman National Forest, Wallowa Mountains Visitors Center, (541) 426-5546

These short but varying routes through the Wallowa Mountain foothills offer stellar views of surrounding mountain ranges, such as the Seven Devils range. The area was changed dramatically after the 1989 Canal fire, a 23,000-acre forest fire that covered much of this area. But what's been left behind is a beautiful study in contrasts. The tall silvery snags, some partially charred to black, make a sort of cool, beautiful contrast against the pure white snow. Beneath these burned veterans, hundreds of upstart trees grow, thick and bushy in the newly provided sun exposure. The burn has also opened up views of the surrounding mountains that might have only been available in quick glimpses before.

All the same, be aware that because many people use these groomed trails, you need to use the usual etiquette when it comes to sharing trails with skiers.

Volunteers and snow travel enthusiasts have built and still maintain a network of developed trails in the Salt Creek Summit area. Volunteers from the Eagle Cap Nordic Club, Wing Ridge Ski Tours, and Wallowa County Gamblers Snowmobile Club have all contributed labor and time to developing this area, including the construction of the log-structure outhouse at the parking lot.

Snowshoers are relative newcomers to the Salt Creek Summit scene,

Wallowa Mountains (Photo by Roger Averbeck/Wing Ridge Ski Tours)

but locals say there's plenty of room. Two routes are described below, although there are several loops to do in this area. Many of them intersect each other at various intervals, and a combination of loops is also possible.

All of them start at the Salt Creek Summit Sno-Park, 12 miles southeast of the town of Joseph on Forest Road 39, which is also called the Hells Canyon Scenic Byway. To get there, drive out of Joseph on the Imnaha Highway 350, and turn right on Forest Road 39. The sno-park is a little more than 7 miles up the winding, intermittently maintained road.

The Summit Loop is one of the easiest trails here, suitable for an afternoon's ramble. The generally flat route showcases the variety of live and dead trees, illustrating the random patterns created in larger forest fires. Start at the trailhead on the west side of the sno-park and head west up a gradual hill. At this point you can go either right or left to do the loop. If you go left, you'll wander more or less to the north, through the woods and a couple of open meadows. In half a mile, come to a junction where turning left keeps you on the shorter loop. A tiny connector trail of less than half a mile turns back to the right, for another junction. To the north of this short loop is a longer loop called the Divide Loop. Take a right here to return to the sno-park in about another half mile.

To do the Mountain View Loop and take in scenes of the Wing Ridge area, leave the Divide Loop and hike north along a flat ridge top that for the most part is open and has great views. Hike another half mile and connect with Forest Road 3915. Follow that north until the trail turns away and to the west. Stay on the 2-mile circuit at the northern end of this route. Finish that and point back the way you came, heading south; connect with the Divide and Summit Loops and back to the sno-park.

--65--
Hurricane Creek

Rating: More difficult
Round trip: 10 miles
Starting elevation: 5,500 feet
High point: 6,000 feet
Best season: March through May
Maps: Imus Geographics, Wallowa Mountains; USGS Chief Joseph Mountain
Who to contact: Wallowa–Whitman National Forest, Wallowa Mountains Visitors Center, (541) 426-5546

While other routes showcase the upper portions of the rugged Wallowa Mountains, this route puts you into the belly of the wilderness. You'll be wandering up a tight canyon with views up, up, and away toward the flanks of dramatic Wallowa Mountain splendor. On this route you may spot some of the elusive mountain goats that live in the area surrounded by the Eagle Cap Wilderness. Some of the tallest and most stunning peaks in the Wallowas rise out of the bottom of this canyon, and the effect can be inspiring (if weather permits any decent views).

Although Hurricane Creek and the campground at the trailhead are heavily used during the summertime, you're likely to have the place to yourself in wintertime. (It's not accessible by snowmobilers.) There isn't much elevation gain to speak of here, but you're surrounded on all sides by some very steep canyon walls, hence the recommended late season. Hurricane Creek didn't get its name from tropical weather patterns, but rather from the appearance of the avalanche-ripped forest after a good storm.

Almost the entire route here is in what avalanche experts consider a "terrain trap." That means that although you won't be walking directly on top of snow that could slide, you're at the bottom of hillsides that might release snow slides during midwinter. The local backcountry ski guide Roger Averbeck of Wing Ridge Tours recommends against doing this

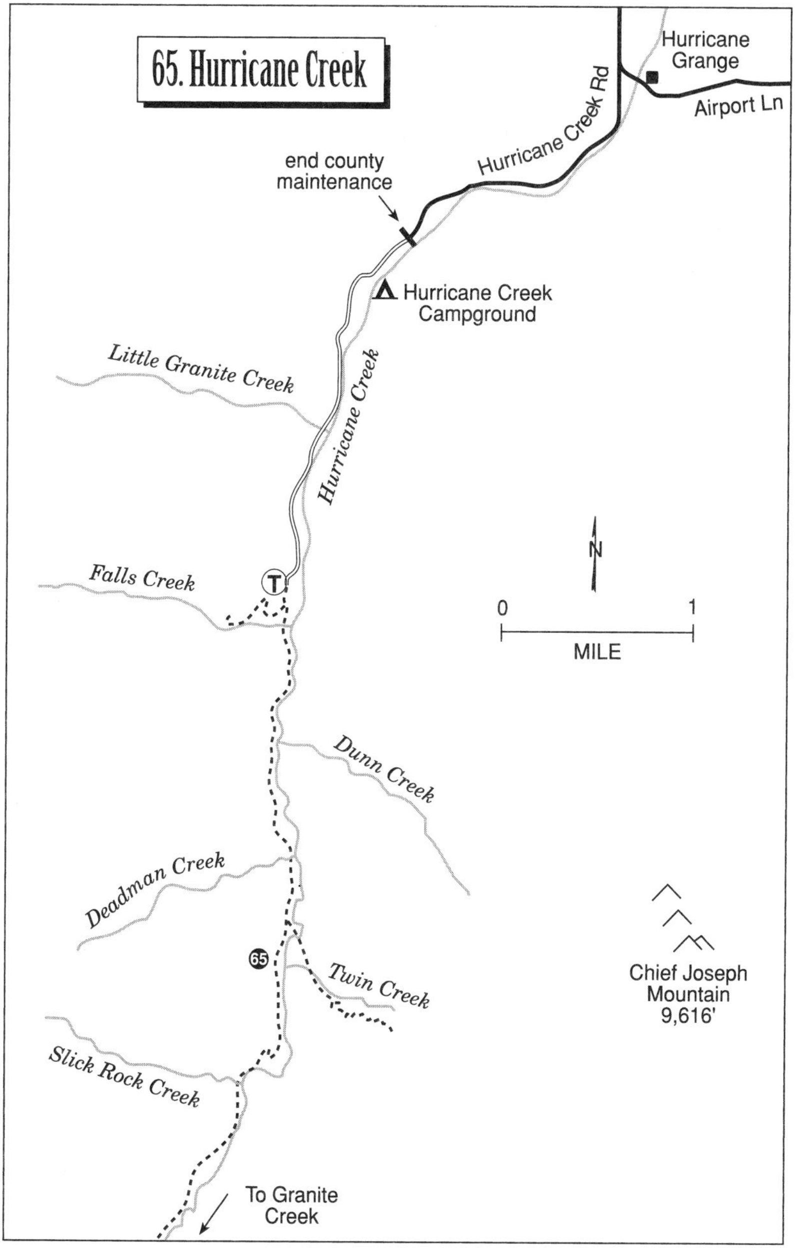
65. Hurricane Creek
Hurricane Grange
Airport Ln
Hurricane Creek Rd
end county maintenance
Hurricane Creek Campground
Little Granite Creek
Hurricane Creek
Falls Creek
T
N
0
1
MILE
Dunn Creek
Deadman Creek
65
Twin Creek
Chief Joseph Mountain 9,616'
Slick Rock Creek
To Granite Creek

route in the midwinter or during and after a heavy snowstorm.

To get there from the charming little town of Joseph, drive west for 3 miles on Airport Lane. After a couple of miles, turn left on Hurricane Creek

Road. It's easy to miss the turnoff for Hurricane Creek Road; watch for the local grange building. The road turns sharply left while Airport Lane gradually curves the other direction.

There isn't much maintenance of the road during the winter, and the county stops doing its work right where the national forest begins. You'll know where that is by the sign, or by the road conditions, or by the sudden absence of home sites along the road. The plowing ends right about at the last driveway, and you might be hard-pressed to go farther if the snow has been heavy that year. Park out of the way if possible, and snowshoe the rest of the road until it turns into the trail. The trailhead to Hurricane Creek is 1.3 miles from the Hurricane Creek Campground.

The route terminates at the trail junction with Granite Creek, signs for which may or may not be visible in heavy snow.

Again, the primary challenge inherent in this route is to be aware and steer clear of avalanche paths. These are most likely to be located in small creek drainages. Always look at the terrain above you and notice the vegetative cover on different hillsides. You'll see that definite avalanche paths have made it hard for trees to establish themselves. Be watchful as you pass beneath these. Some creek drainages, such as Little Granite Creek, have spawned avalanches that have buried the access road.

For the most part, however, this is a great hike in the northeastern Oregon woods. Once at Granite Creek, call it good and head back to the trailhead.

Appendix A

Land Management Agencies

CRATER LAKE NATIONAL PARK
P.O. Box 7
Crater Lake, OR 97604
Phone (541) 594-2211
www.nps.gov/crla/

DESCHUTES NATIONAL FOREST
Headquarters
1645 Highway 20 E
Bend, OR 97701
Phone (541) 383-5300
www.fs.fed.us/r6/centraloregon
Weather report links: *www.fs.fed.us/r6/centraloregon/linkinfo/ weather.html*
Winter recreation: *www.fs.fed.us/r6/centraloregon/recinfo/winterrec/ winterec.html*

Bend/Fort Rock Ranger District
1230 NE 3rd Street, Suite A-262
Bend, OR 97701
Phone: (541) 383-4000

Crescent Ranger District
P.O. Box 208
Crescent, OR 97733
Phone (541) 433-3200

Sisters Ranger District
P.O. Box 249
Sisters, OR 97759
Phone (541) 549-7700

MOUNT HOOD NATIONAL FOREST
Headquarters Office
16400 Champion Way
Sandy, OR 97055
Phone (503) 622-7674
www.fs.fed.us/r6/mthood

Barlow Ranger District
Dufur Ranger Station
780 NE Court Street
Dufur, OR 97021
Phone (503) 467-2291

Bear Springs Work Center
73558 Highway 216
Maupin, OR 97037
Phone (541) 467-2291

Hood River Ranger District
6780 Highway 35
Mount Hood–Parkdale, OR 97041
Phone (541) 352-6002
Trail conditions report: *www.fs.fed.us/r6/mthood*
/trail_condition_report.htm

Zigzag Ranger District
70220 E Highway 26
Zigzag, OR 97049
Phone (541) 622-3191
Winter trails report: *www.fs.fed.us/r6/mthood/zzwtr.htm*

ROGUE RIVER NATIONAL FOREST
Ashland Ranger District
645 Washington Street
Ashland, OR 97520
Phone (541) 482-3333
www.fs.fed.us/r6/rogue/about02.html

UMPQUA NATIONAL FOREST
Diamond Lake Ranger District
2020 Toketee RS Road
Idleyld Park, OR 97447
Phone (541) 498-2531
Diamond Lake snow report: *www.fs.fed.us/r6/umpqua/rec/dlsnow.html*

WALLOWA - WHITMAN NATIONAL FOREST
Wallowa Valley Ranger District
88401 Highway 82
Enterprise, Oregon 97828
Phone (541) 426-4978
www.fs.fed.us/r6/w-w/rog/recrep/recrep_wallowavalley.htm

Wallowa Mountains Visitors Center
Phone (541) 426-5546
www.fs.fed.us/r6/w-w/weekly.htm

WILLAMETTE NATIONAL FOREST
Headquarters
P.O. Box 10607
Eugene, OR 97440
Phone (541) 465-6521
www.fs.fed.us/r6/willamette

Detroit Ranger District
HC73, Box 320
Mill City, OR 97360
Phone (541) 854-3366

McKenzie Ranger District
57600 McKenzie Highway
McKenzie Bridge, OR 97413
Phone (541) 822-3381

Middle Fork Ranger District—Main Office
46375 Highway 58
Westfir, OR 97492
Phone (541) 782-2283

Middle Fork Ranger District—Lowell Office
60 South Pioneer Street
Lowell, OR 97452
Phone (541) 937-2129

WINEMA NATIONAL FOREST
Klamath Ranger District
1936 California Avenue
Klamath Falls, OR 97601
Phone (541) 885-3400
www.fs.fed.us/r6/winema

Appendix B

Sources of Outdoor Recreation Gear and Information

Berg's Ski Shop
13th and Lawrence
Eugene, OR, 97401
Phone (541) 683-1300
www.bergsskishop.com

Hood River Outfitters
1020 Wasco
Hood River, OR 97031
Phone (503) 386-6202

McKenzie Outfitters
1340 Biddle Road
Medford, OR 97504
Phone (541) 773-5145

Mountain Supply
834 NW Colorado Avenue
Bend, OR 97701
Phone (541) 388-0688

Mountain Tracks
69181 E Barlow Trail
Government Camp, OR 97028
Phone (503) 272-3380

Oregon Mountain Community
60 NW Davis
Portland, OR 97209
Phone (503) 227-1038

**Recreational Equipment
Incorporated**
306 Lawrence
Eugene, OR 97401
Phone (541) 465-1800
www.rei.com

Siskiyou Cyclery
1729 Siskiyou Boulevard
Ashland, OR 97520
Phone (541) 482-1997

Skyliner Sports
345 SW Century Drive
Bend, OR 97709
Phone (541) 389-0890

U.S. Outdoor Store
219 SW Broadway Avenue
Portland, OR 97205
Phone (503) 223-5937

Wallowa Outdoors
110 South River Street
Enterprise, OR 97828
Phone (541) 426-3493

Appendix C

Sources of Information about Weather and Snow Conditions

National Weather Service
www.wrh.noaa.gov
Daily forecasts

The Northwest Weather and Avalanche Center
www.nwac.noaa.gov
Provides a forecast for changes in avalanche danger, a detailed summary
of the current snowpack structure and stability, and a 2- or 3-day
forecast of expected weather and its effect on the snowpack structure

Oregon Department of Transportation
Phone (800) 977-ODOT
www.tripcheck.com
The department's travel information website includes "road cams" for
major mountain passes.

The Cyberspace Snow and Avalanche Center
www.csac.org
Provides regularly updated bulletins on snow and avalanche conditions
in the Pacific Northwest

Appendix D

Outdoor Recreation/Conservation Groups and Clubs

The Audubon Society of Portland
5151 NW Cornell Road
Portland OR 97210
Phone (503) 292-6855
Nature store phone (503) 292-9453
www.audubonportland.org

Mazamas
909 NW 19th Avenue
Portland OR 97209
Phone (503) 227-2345
www.mazamas.org

Oregon Chapter Sierra Club
2950 SE Stark, Suite 110
Portland, OR 97214
Phone (503) 238-0442
Fax (503) 238-6281
www.oregon.sierraclub.org

Oregon Natural Resources Council
5825 N Greeley
Portland, OR 97217-4145
Phone (503) 283-6343
Fax (503) 283-0756
www.onrc.org

Index

About the Author

Shea Andersen has been a forest firefighter, a newspaper reporter, and a national park ranger. Born and raised in Portland, Oregon, he is the descendant of an early member of The Snowshoe Club, a group dedicated to mountaineering and good fellowship. He grew up hiking, climbing, and skiing Oregon's Cascades.

Andersen received a master's degree in journalism from the University of Oregon in Eugene. He is a past High Country Fellow through the Institute for Journalism and Natural Resources and is a member of the Society for Environmental Journalists.

Andersen and his wife, Jennifer Pierce, live in Boise, Idaho, where Andersen is a freelance writer and editor. This is his first book.

THE MOUNTAINEERS, founded in 1906, is a nonprofit outdoor activity and conservation club, whose mission is "to explore, study, preserve, and enjoy the natural beauty of the outdoors . . . . " Based in Seattle, Washington, the club is now the third-largest such organization in the United States, with 15,000 members and five branches throughout Washington State.

The Mountaineers sponsors both classes and year-round outdoor activities in the Pacific Northwest, which include hiking, mountain climbing, ski-touring, snowshoeing, bicycling, camping, kayaking and canoeing, nature study, sailing, and adventure travel. The club's conservation division supports environmental causes through educational activities, sponsoring legislation, and presenting informational programs. All club activities are led by skilled, experienced volunteers, who are dedicated to promoting safe and responsible enjoyment and preservation of the outdoors.

If you would like to participate in these organized outdoor activities or the club's programs, consider a membership in The Mountaineers. For information and an application, write or call The Mountaineers, Club Headquarters, 300 Third Avenue West, Seattle, WA 98119; 206-284-6310.

The Mountaineers Books, an active, nonprofit publishing program of the club, produces guidebooks, instructional texts, historical works, natural history guides, and works on environmental conservation. All books produced by The Mountaineers fulfill the club's mission.

Send or call for our catalog of more than 450 outdoor titles:

 The Mountaineers Books
1001 SW Klickitat Way, Suite 201
Seattle, WA 98134
800-553-4453
mbooks@mountaineersbooks.org
www.mountaineersbooks.org

 The Mountaineers Books is proud to be a corporate sponsor of Leave No Trace, whose mission is to promote and inspire responsible outdoor recreation through education, research, and partnerships. The Leave No Trace program is focused specifically on human-powered (non-motorized) recreation.

Leave No Trace strives to educate visitors about the nature of their recreational impacts, as well as offer techniques to prevent and minimize such impacts. Leave No Trace is best understood as an educational and ethical program, not as a set of rules and regulations.

For more information, visit *www.lnt.org*, or call 800-332-4100